SALES PREDICTABILITY

SALES PREDICTABILITY

LEVERAGING ANALYTICS TO SUCCESSFULLY PREDICT BUSINESS RESULTS

DON BECK

SALES PREDICTABILITY
LEVERAGING ANALYTICS TO SUCCESSFULLY PREDICT BUSINESS RESULTS

iUniverse books may be ordered through booksellers or by contacting:

iUniverse
1663 Liberty Drive
Bloomington, IN 47403
www.iuniverse.com
1-800-Authors (1-800-288-4677)

Because of the dynamic nature of the Internet, any web addresses or links contained in this book may have changed since publication and may no longer be valid. The views expressed in this work are solely those of the author and do not necessarily reflect the views of the publisher, and the publisher hereby disclaims any responsibility for them.

Any people depicted in stock imagery provided by Thinkstock are models, and such images are being used for illustrative purposes only.
Certain stock imagery © Thinkstock.

ISBN: 978-1-5320-2302-6 (sc)
ISBN: 978-1-5320-2303-3 (hc)
ISBN: 978-1-5320-2301-9 (e)

Library of Congress Control Number: 2017910023

Print information available on the last page.

iUniverse rev. date: 08/16/2017

CONTENTS

- Percentage of Pipeline Deals Sourced from Marketing
- Percentage of Pipeline Revenue
  Sourced from Marketing
- Win Percentage from Transactions
  Sourced from Marketing
- Marketing Investment per Pipeline Stage
- Marketing Expense as a Percentage of Revenue

- Lead Generation by Program Spending
- Cost per Lead
- Cost of Customer Acquisition (CAC)
- Marketing Velocity

- Days Sales Outstanding (DSO)
- Sales Expense as a Percentage of Revenue
- Average Transaction Size by Rep/Product/Region
- Time Duration to Fully Qualify a Sales Representative
- Average Price per User
- Percentage of Sales Professionals
  Making Annual Quota
- Business Seasonality
- Competitive Analysis—Win/Loss Report
- Product Analysis—Percentage of
  Product Attainment by Quarter
- Cost of Sales Percentage
- Average Discount Rates per Quarter
- Pipeline Aging Ratio by Sales Stage
- Percentage of "No Decision" Losses

- Percentage Attainment during
  the Quarter versus Weekly Targets
- Percentage of Committed Deals (Dollar
  Value) Deferred to Future Quarters
- Pipeline Coverage for Committed
  Quarterly Forecast by Sales Stage
- Close to Pipeline Ratio (Quality
  Pipeline or Lack of Rep Coverage)
- Pipeline by Sales Stage versus Committed Forecast
- Percentage of the Forecast Change
  versus Commitment—Weekly Variance
- Average Sell Cycle by Product or Target Market

To my family. My wife, Suzy, has stood by me for many years regardless of the sacrifices associated with my career aspirations. She has always been the foundation of our wonderful family, and I am very fortunate to have her in my life. My three children, Lindsay, Danny, and Ryan, are the source of my inspiration. I strive every day to make them proud. I could not have accomplished a thing in my career without their support. I am truly a blessed man.

PREFACE

Your reputation is more important than your paycheck, and your integrity is worth more than your career.
                    —Ryan Freitas, About.me cofounder

So why write a book about sales predictability? Why is it important for sales and marketing leadership to embrace the importance of forecast accuracy in their daily responsibilities? It is simple. Nobody likes surprises, especially in business.

A sales forecast is a business commitment. You are putting your professional reputation on the line that you will deliver on your forecast promise. Executives who miss these business commitments on a consistent basis typically lose their jobs. I saw this all the time in the tech industry of Silicon Valley. It doesn't matter how polished your sales presentation skills are or even your leadership qualities. By missing your forecast commitments on a regular basis, you are demonstrating a complete lack of visibility into your business. It drives senior leadership crazy and in almost all cases will not be tolerated. This includes falling short of your forecast as well as dramatically exceeding your own projections. If you think overachieving your forecast instills confidence in your senior manager, then you are wrong. And this mistake can lead to the termination of your employment. All you are doing is clearly communicating to senior management that you have no clue how to predict business results. Again, nobody likes surprises, especially your employer.

I have seen many talented sales and marketing executives lose their jobs because they did not understand the dynamics of their business and could not communicate accurate sales forecasts on a regular basis. Successful sales leadership is measured by business results. It sounds simple and oversimplifies the vast responsibilities of a sales executive, but it really comes down to this basic success criteria. C-level executives have confidence in their sales executives when they make their assigned revenue targets on a consistent basis. Great sales leaders hold themselves as well as their team to a higher level of accountability. They understand the importance of adhering to strict process disciplines in managing the sales and marketing opportunities of the company. That is also why the very best sales leaders are also driven by data as a proof point for the effectiveness and efficiency of their sales and marketing teams. This focus on predictive analytics drives better decision making, leading to stronger business results.

This is why this book is so important. It is basically a playbook with which to manage the revenue cycle of your company from marketing lead generation to predicting when key transactions will close. Companies live or die by their ability to predict the future. Wall Street rewards public companies that consistently meet or exceed quarterly revenue and profit projections. Missed revenue projections send the message to Wall Street that the company does not have the required visibility into its business. It lowers shareholder confidence in the company. But this issue is not limited just to public companies. Private companies have a board of directors that holds their CEOs to the same level of accountability. CEOs are exposed when business results differ dramatically from committed business projections.

And the first to be blamed will always be sales management.

The objective of this book is to focus on the science of selling and the process of maximizing the predictability of the sales cycle. It will include best practices in forecast techniques and a variety of sales tools that will assist in the process of predicting sales results on a consistent basis. It also includes a portfolio of key performance indicators that will provide greater insight into your sales and marketing pipeline.

Regardless of the size of your team, as a sales or marketing manager you are now responsible for the expertise and professionalism of your sales organization. Any issues or concerns with your team's performance will be a reflection of your leadership. This is a daunting task and not one that anyone should take lightly. This book will provide valuable tips and techniques to help you manage your sales and marketing organization and improve your team's ability to honor its business commitments on a consistent basis.

Since I spent my entire career in the technology industry, the examples in this book may have an emphasis on software and technology industry challenges. Even though there is an emphasis on a specific industry, I am confident that the concepts and best practices can be transferred to any size company and in any industry scenario. Included in this book are multiple examples of sales tools and process discipline documentation that will be extremely valuable in managing the sales and marketing engagement process of your organization. It is recommended that you take these examples and tailor them to your specific business or industry sector.

I hope you find this content informative and extremely valuable in addressing your most challenging sales leadership endeavors.

INTRODUCTION

Ideas are easy. Implementation is hard.
—Guy Kawasaki,
Alltop cofounder and entrepreneur

The profession of sales and marketing management is both an art and a science.

The art aspect is the expertise of the sales executive in articulating the business value of his or her solution and how it impacts the business results of the end customer. It includes building relationships with your prospective customers and business partners. It is about earning their trust and confidence in your company's solution. It is also about earning the right to be called a trusted adviser to your clients. This is never easy and includes not only an in-depth understanding of your company's product and its salient features but also how your solution will impact your prospective customers' business.

It is also an aspect of your overall professionalism within your current employer. It is not just about achieving your quota targets. It is also important that you produce your results the right way. Integrity, ethics, and strong business values are requirements for any sales leader. Success here will ensure you have earned credibility with not only your customers and business partners but also your employer. Your expertise will distinguish you as a skilled sales executive, and your employer will value your contributions.

The science aspect of sales management is very different and in many ways far more challenging to master. The science aspect of sales management is maximizing the visibility into the sales cycle to effectively and efficiently manage sales engagements to close on time. It includes analyzing the trends associated with important key performance indicators to gain insight into the performance of your team and the dynamics of the pipeline. In many ways, it is making the necessary investments to understand the past in order to predict the future.

With so much on the line, it is astonishing how many companies do not use predictive analytics to improve their accuracy with sales forecasts. Twenty-five years ago, sales and marketing organizations embraced sales force automation as a means to standardize and provide consistency to the sales engagement process. This greatly helped preliminary understanding of the dynamics of the sales and marketing process. But this investment is not enough.

All companies actively pursue the quest for *predictable, profitable revenue growth*. Your job as the senior leader of sales and marketing is to deliver these predictable results for your company. Your employer is dependent on your ability to not only make your quarterly business objectives but predict the outcome of the quarter on a consistent basis. In certain industries, failure at either of these tasks could lead to your termination. That is the fact of life as a sales executive. High stress is just a part of the job. You live your life over quarterly increments. If you make your numbers this quarter, then you live to keep your job for another ninety days. This is the cold, hard truth of the sales profession in many industries. The key to your professionalism as a sales executive is to be accurately predictable with your business commitments.

All three components (predictability, profitability, and growth) represent their own challenges. Growing revenues with profitability requires the efforts of the entire company. But sales predictability typically falls on the shoulders of the sales and marketing leadership team. These executives are responsible for the visibility into the sales pipeline and predicting the transaction flow for the company. It does not matter if the company is privately held or a publically traded entity. The professionalism of any sales and marketing executive is tied to his or her success in producing business results—the integrity of the transactions sold and the visibility into the business to accurately predict when sales engagements will close and revenue is recognized. Forecast accuracy is a critical component of a sales executive's responsibility.

The key attributes that C-level executives look for in their sales and marketing leadership have a great deal to do with sales predictability. They want executives who do the following:

- Understand their top deals for the quarter in detail, including where each opportunity is in the sell cycles and the keys to winning over the competition. They will look to you for revenue guidance in the quarter each and every week.
- Have personal involvement in the key transactions. In theory, the senior sales and marketing leader should be the top sales talent in the company. C-level executives are more confident in deals where you are personally involved and have a relationship with the senior executives of the prospective customer. They like when you get your hands dirty.

- Know the strengths and weaknesses of the sales and marketing team. They look for senior leadership to leverage the strengths and minimize the weaknesses of the team with top engagements.
- Set the tone for the sales and marketing team for execution excellence and accountability. It gives C-level executives great confidence when the company's value proposition is presented consistently and professionally across all sales and marketing personnel. His or her leadership makes the company look good!

Sales and marketing leadership that invest in predictive analytics outperform those who don't recognize the value of these measurements. Predictive analytics provides critical visibility into the business operations of sales and marketing operations. This can lead to critical decisions that will lift revenue projections. Sales and marketing leadership can leverage analytics to better understand profitable industry segments. It can also help assess what is required to penetrate new markets. Most importantly, the use of predicative analytics by the sales and marketing organization can enhance their understanding of the buying habits of their valued client targets.

Knowledge is truly powerful with forecast accuracy.

CHAPTER 1

STRATEGIC CLARITY AND SETTING EXPECTATIONS

Data beats emotions.
—Sean Rad, Adly and Tinder founder

There is a strong link between the success with forecast accuracy of your sales organization and the team's understanding on what is expected from their roles and responsibilities for the company. This applies to all sales resources both internal and external. Sales and marketing management need to overcommunicate what is expected in every aspect of their team's daily responsibilities. This includes their complete commitment to adhering to the process disciplines associated with sales predictability. The first step is to ensure your entire sales and marketing team clearly understands the corporate strategy of the company.

- Are the strategic imperatives of the company clearly understood within the sales organization?
- Do members of the sales team understand the importance of their specific contributions to the success of the company?

- Are expectations properly set? Is it understood within the sales organization that although revenue generation is important, the quality of the transactions is equally important? Does transactional integrity permeate the entire sales organization?
- Is accountability established and embraced by every member of the sales and marketing team?
- Are process disciplines, so critical for sales predictability, in place today?

It is imperative that every company establishes corporate strategy clarity for all its employees, but this is extremely important for sales and marketing resources. Before we go into details on specific sales and marketing tasks surrounding forecast accuracy, let's discuss the importance of corporate strategy clarity to setting a foundation for predictability with sales results.

This lesson was learned back when I was with IBM and Lou Gerstner joined as president and CEO. IBM was struggling and hemorrhaging money back in the early nineties. He was pressured for a decision to either keep IBM whole as a company or break it into multiple independent companies. Employees were sailors on a rudderless ship. We wanted to be led and were looking for a senior leader to show us the path to success. Mr. Gerstner received great notoriety when he said that the last thing IBM needed then was a vision. He went on to say that what IBM needed right then was a series of very tough-minded, market-driven, highly effective strategies in each of its businesses. These strategies had to be completely embraced by all employees.

He then laid out the following strategic imperatives that all IBM employees must adhere to in their daily work activities:

- The marketplace is the driving force behind everything we do.
- At our core, we are a technology company with an overriding commitment to quality.
- Our primary measures of success are customer satisfaction and shareholder value.
- We operate as an entrepreneurial organization with a minimum of bureaucracy and a never-ending focus on productivity.
- We never lose sight of our strategic vision.
- We think and act with a sense of urgency.
- Outstanding, dedicated people make it all happen, particularly when they work together as a team.
- We are sensitive to the needs of all employees and to the communities in which we operate.

All performance plans, development plans, and compensation plans clearly supported this focus. Although Mr. Gerstner did not have sales predictability in mind when he established these strategic imperatives, it set the tone for the necessary discipline and accountability critical for success with this endeavor.

His passion was also clear to all employees. He instilled a sense of urgency in all IBM employees to work together toward creating greater value for our clients. Mr. Gerstner established the importance of teamwork and collaboration, which will be a consistent message throughout this book for sales predictability.

Mr. Gerstner went on to say that the fundamental problem at IBM was a lack of focus, execution, and accountability. Again, focus, execution, and accountability are also critical for sales predictability. Some companies do this better than others. The best do it extremely well. This book will focus on what is required to be successful with this critical endeavor.

All sales documentation (job descriptions, performance plans, compensation plans, quota assignments, etc.) must clearly support your company achieving these corporate objectives. All employees at IBM at the time knew that the company's priorities established by our CEO were not going to change. We knew that our goals and objectives for the year were also not going to change.

Our strategic imperatives were clear and concise, and every employee in the company could recite his or her role and responsibilities in contributing to the company's strategic imperatives. It made all our jobs easier and contributed to better business results and happier employees.

For sales representatives, it is important that they make their business commitments (quota attainment) to the company, but how they accomplish these goals is equally important. The last thing a company wants are sales personnel who sign poor deals and bring minimal profits into the company, all the while padding their commission checks.

This is one of the prime reasons the sales profession has a very poor reputation in some companies. You may have heard the term "coin operated" as a reference to sales personnel. I hate that term since it implies that all sales people are only in the job for the money and will put their interests ahead of what is best for the company. I have had the good fortune to work with some of the best and brightest in the sales profession in the high-tech industry. The common trait among these individuals was that they were professional and always put the company first. The more the company succeeded, the more financial rewards were available to all company personnel.

I also expected each member of the sales organization to conduct business with the highest ethics and integrity. To ensure every member of the team understood the importance of doing quality business the right way, I published *expectation documents* annually for each employee in the sales organization. So at the beginning of every year, members of the sales team would receive their annual quota, a compensation plan, and their expectation document.

Let's review the components of an expectation document. Expectation documents provide critical clarity. For example, the use of this customer relationship management (CRM) tool has always been a condition of employment for all sales resources in my organization. Let's start with some definitions of what I mean with this valuable sales tool. In the high-tech world, CRM has been critical to the success of sales predictability of any company. CRM is also too often confused with sales force automation (SFA), a system used to track deals and report to management. CRM is bigger and more comprehensive, encompassing sales, service, and marketing. As social media began to grab the limelight, people began to take another look at CRM, leading to a new concept called *social CRM*. For the purpose of this book, we will refer to the required tools for managing the entire revenue cycle of a company as customer relationship management (CRM).

If only 70 percent of the sales personnel used the CRM tool and that was the basis of my revenue forecast to the business, then I would at best be only 70 percent accurate with my business commitments. This has to be explained to all sales resources in the company. If they did not adhere to this requirement, then they were subject to dismissal from the company. No exceptions.

Another good example is a side letter certification. A side letter is defined as any contingency to the transaction that would affect revenue recognition. This could be a commitment for price protection, an agreement to refund money if expectations were not met, or any future commitment to product functionality or concessions that were instrumental to the sale in the current quarter. For a publicly traded company, this could potentially lead to restating the books. When that happens, senior leadership typically lose their jobs, including the head of sales. The penalty is not as severe with private companies, but it still could lead to the termination of sales leadership. In either case, it is a reflection of the professionalism in the sales organization.

That is why I spent so much time compiling expectation documents. I wanted everybody in the organization to be considered true professionals and clearly understand what was expected of them on a daily basis. You will see that this role and responsibility clarity is vital for forecast accuracy. I will share the document I used to establish clarity for the roles and responsibilities of each member of the sales team and why each section of this document is important.

Here is an example of an expectation document for a field sales representative and an explanation of the importance of each section:

Date: January 15th, 20XX
To: Sales Account Manager—North America Enterprise Sales Team
From: Regional Sales Directors—North America
Subject: Sales Account Manager/Field Sales Expectations Document

The purpose of this document is to outline sales activity expectations for North American Sales Account Managers. It is a listing of required activities that are fundamental to the success of each Sales Account Manager (AM) and therefore the success of the company. It is expected that the AM can adequately document their achievements with these required activities.

1. Consistent Revenue Attainment

The primary responsibility of the Sales Account Manager is to generate net new revenue opportunities from both current and prospective customers as well as to manage their overall customer satisfaction with our company. Each Account Manager is expected to meet or exceed their quarterly quota. It is the top priority of each Account Manager. Success with sales execution comes down to process discipline, strategic clarity, and a high performance culture. The success of the North American Solution Sales organization will be primarily measured by our quarterly and annual attainment across all products in 20XX. It is acceptable to substantially exceed revenue expectations in one product line, but sales should be balanced across all product lines while exceeding annual targets. The expectations for 20XX are as follows:

- meet or exceed quarterly and annual revenue objectives (100 percent of assigned objectives)

- meet or exceed quarterly and annual product targets (100 percent of assigned objectives)
- achieve productivity per head count by quarter (goal of approximately $500K of total revenue per quarter for at least two quarters of the year)
- grow average transaction size and number of deals over $50K each quarter

Why this section is important: First and foremost, you establish a clear goal for the year in regards to revenue attainment on a consistent basis. Making your assigned quota is important, but this document stresses the importance of consistent performance and contribution to the business. The reference to customer satisfaction is important because it is a strategic imperative of our company. Selling your products and services should be done in a professional manner so that customer satisfaction is paramount to all your sales activities. You will also see that two key performance indicators have been assigned to each rep: average transaction size and number of quarterly deals. Success with these measurements can happen only if they are reviewed with each sales rep on a consistent basis.

2. Compliance with Company's Sales Empowerment Grid

All sales personnel must adhere to the guidelines published in the company's Empowerment Grid. This means all transactions must follow the discounting parameters as documented within the Empowerment Grid. This document also provides process disciplines for contract-signing authority as well as other deal-related guidelines such as credit and contract terms.

Why this section is important: What is a sales empowerment grid? It provides clear guidelines on what a sales representative is empowered to offer a customer in regard to discounting parameters as well as contractual flexibility. The objective of the empowerment grid is to ensure that your sales personnel are viewed by the customer as an extension of the company and that he or she is empowered to structure deal parameters and make concessions without permission from senior management. The professionalism of the sales organization can have a significant impact on customer satisfaction. Effective deployment of a well-documented sales empowerment grid can be instrumental to shortening sales cycles. Please refer to chapter 9, "Sales Tools," for an example of a sales empowerment grid.

3. Collaboration with Marketing to Build a Quality Pipeline

Critical to ensuring sales predictability and consistent revenue attainment is establishing a pipeline that ensures the required coverage to meet your quota objectives. To be successful with this initiative, it is imperative to work closely with your field-marketing colleagues to build a quality pipeline. The AM is expected to work with marketing to build a pipeline that is 3X to 4X their monthly, quarterly, and annual business commitments. This is necessary for exceeding quota and establishing forecast accuracy and predictability. It is expected that marketing will generate 60 percent of your pipeline, and sales personnel will be responsible for the remaining 40 percent of the required pipeline. This objective will not be possible without strong teamwork and collaboration between sales and marketing resources. This is a common goal of both organizations. Key performance indicators include:

- pipeline coverage of outlook commitment/annual quota (goal: 3X–4X)
- ensure quality pipeline and coverage for current and next quarter (at least two-quarter view must be presented on a regular basis)
- pipeline by sales stage (pipeline should have 35 percent of all quarterly opportunities from the committed outlook in sales stage 5–7)

Why this section is important: This section stresses the importance of teamwork and collaboration between sales and marketing organizations for a common. goal of building a quality pipeline. It clearly specifies pipeline coverage for deals and revenue of 3X the associated quota assignment. It is clear to all sales personnel that you will inspect a two-quarter review of this measurement and that the pipeline must reflect quality opportunities in each sales stage.

4. Consistent Use of Salesforce.com for Deal Visibility

Each Account Manager is expected to use Salesforce.com to identify and track all opportunities. Salesforce.com usage is considered a condition of employment within the North American Solution Sales organization. The 20XX Compensation Plans require that all sales opportunities be entered and managed in the Salesforce.com system in order to receive commissions or quota credit. This must be completed in a timely manner and should be reviewed weekly with your manager. Each AM is expected to know the details of every proposed transaction in their pipeline for the current quarter and at least one quarter out. The expectations for 20XX are as follows:

- Salesforce.com updates per week by AM (goal: 3–5 minimum per day or as required).
- Salesforce.com records must be completely accurate for current quarter and at least one quarter out.
- By week 2 of each quarter, your current-quarter Salesforce.com records are completely accurate, and your current quarter forecast has been established.

Why this section is important: First of all, it does not matter what customer relationship management (CRM) tool is used for this measurement. I have extensive experience with Salesforce.com, and that is the only reason it is referenced in this document. The reason the use of this tool is considered a condition of employment is that you will not be able to reach deal visibility or forecast accuracy without the commitment of your entire team. I can't stress the importance of this requirement enough. Do not hesitate to take termination action if any employee in your organization is not completely committed to this objective. Remember that your professionalism with sales predictability will be a reflection of how committed your team is to this task.

5. Forecasting Accuracy

Each AM is expected to forecast accurately on a consistent basis. This requires each deal to be tracked and moved through the normal pipeline steps as defined in the Salesforce.com system. Each AM must be knowledgeable on the progress toward completeness of each proposed transaction and have the necessary information to show that a deal is moving through the pipeline. And ultimately, as deals are forecasted, each Account Manager should be certain that these deals will close in the quarter in which they are forecasted. Key performance indicators:

- forecast accuracy by quarter (goal: 10 percent variance from week 6 to final commitment—week 10 variance will not exceed 1–3 percent)

Why this section is important: This measurement assumes you are tracking your monthly and quarterly outlook each week with a forecast and pipeline review. By week 6 of the quarter, you should be asking for a firm forecast and a commitment to a revenue outlook. This forecast should not vary more than 10 percent between week 6 and the close of the quarter. The same applies to the week-10 committed forecast. This should not vary by more than 3 percent. By communicating your expectations, it makes it clear the importance you are putting on forecast accuracy for your team. This also should be reflected in the assigned compensation plan as well as the annual performance review process.

6. Target and Contact

It is imperative that each Account Manager has a proactive target and contact plan for executives in their named accounts. This requires that each Account Manager adequately maps each named account and targets specific executives via target and contact calls or marketing campaigns. The expectations for 20XX are as follows:

- minimum of five target and contact account calls per week to new executives in the Account Manager's named account portfolio

Why this section is important: This measurement makes it clear that you can't count on marketing to provide all the leads necessary to make your number. It is the responsibility of every sales representative to make specific contributions to his or her respective pipeline. These meetings should be monitored during the weekly pipeline reviews to ensure the objectives of the meetings were met and an action plan is in place.

7. No Side Letter Agreements

At the end of every quarter, each AM must certify that his or her transactions closed did not have any written or implied side letter agreement in place. A side letter is defined as any contingency to the transaction that would affect revenue recognition. This could be price protection, an agreement to refund money if expectations were not met, or any future commitment to product functionality or concessions that were instrumental to the sale in the current quarter. This could potentially lead to restating the books, and the avoidance of this unacceptable behavior is also considered a condition of employment within the sales organization.

- no side letter certification at the end of each quarter

Why this section is important: This is to ensure that all deals are clean and that no sales representative makes a private commitment to close a deal that could jeopardize revenue recognition at the end of a quarter. This applies more to public companies, but it is also a reflection of the professionalism of any sales organization.

8. Solution Selling Expertise

Each Account Manager should be able to demonstrate a thorough and complete understanding of the company's enterprise solution positioning. This expertise includes knowledge of the company's value proposition and competitive positioning in the market. Included in this requirement is a clear understanding of your customer's business and how the company's enterprise solution portfolio can generate greater customer value. The expectations for 20XX are as follows:

*   All Account Managers certified on required enterprise messaging and content.
*   Demonstrate your knowledge of our enterprise value proposition specific to a targeted industry vertical.
*   Contribute deals each quarter to the WIN reports and reference program.

Why this section is important: While we will concentrate on the science aspect of sales predictability, let's not forget the importance of the art aspect of sales excellence. Strategic clarity also extends to how your team can articulate your company's value proposition. To ensure that strategic clarity has permeated the entire sales organization from a content and messaging standpoint, you must ask yourself the following questions:

1. Can your sales team clearly articulate your company's strategy at any time?
2. Is the company strategy described the same way regardless of who is asked within your sales organization?

3. Do all decisions and actions within the sales organization reflect this commitment to the company strategy?
4. Does everybody within the sales organization, including business partners, know the importance of his or her contribution to the company strategy?
5. Does everybody on your sales team believe in the company strategy and have confidence in his or her ability to contribute to its success?

The answer to these questions can make a huge difference in the success or failure of your sales efforts for the fiscal year. Morale is directly tied to the confidence that a salesperson has in his or her ability to contribute to the success of the company. Morale is also tied to clear priorities that do not change throughout the year. Stress is caused when personal work efforts and labor are not tied to the priorities of the company. This could lead to higher than acceptable attrition among the sales personnel. Strategic ambiguity can destroy the cultural fabric of any company. As the leader of the sales organization, it is your responsibility to ensure that strategic clarity permeates your entire organization and is the driving motivation behind every decision and all actions from your team.

1. Build and Execute a Territory/Account/Opportunity Plans

Each Account Manager is required to build and execute a territory plan for their named accounts. This requires working with the Field Marketing personnel as well as the regional Partner/Channel Manager to include key demand generation and marketing activities. The expectations for 20XX are as follows:

- Territory plans should be completed and reviewed by management no later than February 15th, 20XX
- Account Plans should also be completed for your top revenue opportunity each quarter. This should occur no later than the end of the first month of the quarter.

Why this section is important: For large account opportunities where your team manages a complex sell cycle with a Fortune 500 company, it is recommended that your team build a territory or account plan that is reviewed and approved by management. Please refer to chapter 9, "Sales Tools," for an example of a territory and account plan template.

2. Build and Execute a Channel/Partner Account Plan

Each Account Manager is required to build and execute a partner attack plan for their territory. This includes working with the Regional Partner/Channel Manager and the Regional Sales Director to identify key channel partners in the geographic area that can be a critical success factor in aiding the AM in attaining their quota. Additionally, a call plan needs to be developed and executed for engaging with partners. The expectations for 20XX are as follows:

- Partner plans for 20XX should be completed and reviewed by management no later than February 30th, 20XX.

Why this section is important: If your business has a channel component to your sales model that makes sure there is a formal partner plan in place, it should address all aspects of channel strategy, including recruitment, management, and retention investments.

Questions regarding any of these performance expectations should be directed to your Regional Sales Director for clarification.

Please sign below acknowledging that you have read and understand the expectations for success in this role.

_____   _____
Account Manager Signature   Date

_____   _____
Regional Sales Manager Signature   Date

Why joint signature is important: This is a formal agreement with you and each member of your sales team. You need complete commitment from each member to adhere to these guidelines in order to have the right to be a part of your sales organization. It is a key measurement tool for ensuring that each member of your team has the professionalism you expect at your company.

This is just an example of a sales expectation document and not for everybody to replicate exactly. This was for sales personnel, but a similar document can be built for your marketing resources as well. You can tailor this document to any job description within your organization, and it should reflect the five to ten most important aspects you value as the leader of the sales and marketing organization. If this document is well written and managed correctly, then you will find your team referencing its content throughout the year. It should also be a key mechanism for annual performance reviews.

It should be distributed with a compensation plan and quota assignment as early in the year as possible, preferably the first week of January. Your compensation structure and communications should be consistent with both the overall strategy of the company and the expectation documentation. An entire book could be dedicated to the importance of aligning compensation plans to the strategic imperatives of the company. There are many facets to building a pay-for-performance culture at a company.

The best sales representatives are sales plan lawyers in that they can scrutinize every aspect of their compensation plan and deduct what is the strategic direction of the company. That only happens when the compensation plan is clearly written and reflects the priorities of the company.

It is important to include representatives from all job disciplines within the sales organization to participate in the process of designing the compensation plan for the year. This helps secure the necessary commitment from the field sales personnel that the plan is fair and equitable. I also include representatives from human resources to ensure that it reflects the best interest of the company, and members of the finance team to ensure the plan is equitable and affordable.

It is important that you have alignment within the sales organization on five components of the compensation plan and its philosophy for the year. These five components are as follows:

1. Sales Plan Eligibility

- Determine sales plan eligibility within the sales organization.
- Limited to positions with direct impact on closing individual sales (this can include business development, solution engineering, or account management).

2. Earnings Opportunity and Leverage

- Show market research that highlights on-target earnings (OTE) that reflect competitive market median for positions with similar responsibilities and requiring similar skills, experience, and competencies.
- Highlight how compensation components (base salary and incentive/commission) are fair and equitable within the industry.
- Total earnings potential projected in top quartile of market for "excellent" results. This shows that top performers will be the top earners and the basic philosophy of the compensation plan is to "reward the doers."
- Plan downside/deceleration proportionate to plan upside and reflective of impact on results. This is fair to the company. Lack of business contributions should have a penalty, much as top performers have a reward. This is where thresholds or a minimum quota attainment to achieve an incentive payment must be evaluated. This could also include linkages where an incentive payment is tied to achieving one goal before paying on another goal.
- Pay mix (base salary versus incentive variable) reflects the degree of persuasion applied in closing individual sales.

The best sales representatives want the most leverage and typically request a 50 percent base and 50 percent incentive plan. Presales engineers (solution engineers or SEs) typically look for a 70/30 percent plan since they do not have as much direct influence on the sale. Having representatives from each job discipline within sales will help in building a plan that is right for all job descriptions. External resources can assist with assessing market-competitive salary components.

- Other variables to consider are the length of the sell cycle, the complexity of the solution offering, and if a services component is a critical part of the sale.

3. Metrics and Weightings

- This measurement should be reflective of the sales representative role in delivering on the imperatives of your company's specific strategy. For example, your company may want sales representatives to push a new product introduction and will put added incentives to achieve sales in this area.
- Weightings based on desired prioritization—balancing core revenue generation with strategic products and objectives. Will measurements be based on revenue or profit contributions? How is the commission incentive tied to the goals and objectives of the company? Will it incent the right behavior for the sales organization? A great example is establishing incentives for organic business growth from existing customers versus net new business from new customer prospects.

4. Plan Frequency/Performance Period

- Frequency (monthly, quarterly, semiannually) dependent on length of sales cycle. For example, inside sales representatives (telesales) typically have smaller deal sizes with shorter associated sell cycles. These individuals usually have their commission payments conducted monthly, whereas field sales personnel have larger deals in their pipeline with longer sell cycles. These individuals have their commission payments done quarterly.

5. Quota Setting

- Individual quotas are set to reflect expected business performance with an expectation that 70 percent of reps achieve quota when the business achieves expected results. The model assumes overachievement from some sales representatives that offset the underachievement of others. If too many sales representatives overachieve their annual business objectives, then the commission structure may not be affordable for the business results generated. If your company is not paying the allocated commissions for the month/quarter, then the quota assignments may be too high.
- Individual quotas reflect differences in target-addressable markets within and across roles. For example, inside sales representatives (telesales) more often are focused on small and medium business prospects and have average transaction sizes significantly less than their direct sales counterparts. The quotas should obviously be smaller relative to enterprise field representatives in order to reflect the role and responsibilities of the inside sales representative and their target market (small and medium businesses).

It is important to reiterate that one size does not fit all when it comes to compensation plans. A great deal of sales plan variation can be due to the stage of the company. For example, a start-up will have very different incentive components compared to a large, publically traded company.

Start-ups are looking for traction in the market and should reward their sales personnel for landing significant customers who will provide credibility to the company. These early customers are critical for references, and the incentives should reward this success. Compensation is typically associated with low base pay but heavy commission weighting toward new business.

As a company grows, the incentive plan should reflect growth parameters. New customer incentives and user growth will be critical to the success of the company at this stage. Major incentives could be tied to revenue growth (not necessarily profit) or customer acquisition.

As the company matures, the incentives can transition to profit-based metrics such as profit margin and discounting disciplines. Maximizing profit contributions for sales reflects not only on the stage of the company but the professionalism of the sales force. Typically a more experienced sales organization will be recruited to a mature company that requires a significant base and variable pay component. The sales skills required for mature companies reflect a unique industry or product expertise and a higher level of professionalism that comes with experience.

As the company branches out into new markets, the compensation plan needs to reflect this new corporate direction. Launching new products into an existing customer base is a good example of this next phase of compensation leverage for your sales personnel. This is where "hunters" and "farmers" have different roles within a company to maximize the effectiveness of the sales resource investment.

So it is important to note that commission plans tailored for your sales team today might not be what is needed to achieve the company's strategic goals in the future.

Some important tips when designing a sales compensation plan:

1. Sales personnel like things simple and straightforward. Do not make the plan too complex or have a significant administrative element to burden the team.
2. Make sure the compensation plan reflects the degree of difficulty of the sales expertise. For example, sophisticated solution sales representatives should be paid more than renewal sales personnel, who are more transactional, or fulfillment sales.
3. A good sales plan will both attract and retain your talent. Take the time to do it right.
4. Make sure accelerators for overachievement are tightly aligned to the goals and objectives of the company. It is equally important to include language that management reserves the right to make any adjustments in the best interest of the company. I can assure you that this language will not be popular with the sales team, but it is necessary to protect the company for overpayments tied to "bluebirds" or a large transaction that happened and required little or no sales effort to close. To secure the trust of the sales team, it is critical that the leadership

team does not mismanage this compensation clause. It is insurance that the compensation plan will be judged fairly by both the sales team and management.

5.   Ensure conflict resolution guidelines are incorporated into the compensation plan. When a sales representative feels that his or her payout is not fair, ensure that there are escalation procedures to accomplish a fair and equitable resolution.

6.   Show examples of how much compensation is available for scenarios at 100 percent, 125 percent, and 150 percent of quota attainment.

7.   Don't pay sales personnel unless their customers pay their bills. Customers who are consistent Accounts Receivable problems are rarely worth the effort. Your sales personnel should not benefit from a bad customer.

8.   Incorporate profit and discounting disciplines into the compensation plans as much as possible. This discipline will improve your team's professionalism.

9.   When modifying a compensation plan from one year to another, always overcommunicate the changes and explain in detail the business justification and motivation of the decision.

10. Always include forecast accuracy as a key component of your sales incentive plan.

Follow these guidelines to ensure you have a sales compensation plan that is designed to meet the goals and objectives of your company. Each year, the compensation plan and expectation document should be updated to reflect current priorities and distributed to all sales personnel as early in the year as possible. Special meetings should be conducted to ensure every member of the team understands each component of the documentation. These meetings should also stress the importance of adhering to these guidelines. Again, the professionalism of your team reflects your professionalism. If your team misses forecasts or signs bad deals, it is a direct reflection on your leadership.

CHAPTER 2

GO-TO-MARKET CONSIDERATIONS

Anything that is measured and watched, improves.
—Bob Parsons, GoDaddy founder

The goal of any go-to-market strategy is to maximize your revenue attainment with the most effective and efficient cost of sales labor. This chapter will address the decisions necessary to build the proper sales organization structure critical for success.

This is a topic that is very broad and complex, and the content in this chapter is focused on the lessons learned from the enterprise software industry and may not apply to all market sectors. As a sales and marketing executive for close to thirty-six years, I was responsible for making resource investments that were tailored to the buying behaviors of my prospective customers as well as the overall strategy of my company. Many issues must be addressed before a sound go-to-market strategy is developed that will accelerate the success of your company's strategy.

A few of these issues are as follows:

1. Target market segmentation: enterprise (Fortune 500), midmarket, small and medium business, small office / home office (SOHO)
2. Channel leverage
3. Industry segmentation
4. User experience of your product or services
5. Business model

Let's discuss each topic in more detail.

1. Target Market

Market segmentation is critical to aligning the sales and marketing resources in your organization to the business opportunities being pursued by your business. If you offer a highly complex product or service and are focused primarily on Fortune 500 enterprise customers, then it is most likely that you will need to invest in direct field sales personnel.

This is not a decision that any organization should take lightly. These are the most expensive sales resources a company can invest in, and it is extremely important that an organization does its homework and understands the implications of this decision. This investment is typically required when personal interaction via face-to-face meetings with the economic buyer of your solution is required. Many times it is associated with a lengthy and complex sell cycle with a large price tag. Mostly these companies have well over 2,500 employees and multiple domestic and international offices that add complexity to the selling process.

Securing large transactions from prominent Fortune 500 companies can be a boost to your market presence. Their logo can appear on your web page to add credibility to your company. But these deals can also lead to interesting challenges. Prominent companies know their impact and leverage during both initial and ongoing contract negotiations. It is not uncommon to secure a key transaction with a prominent company only to be held hostage at renewal time for deeper discounts or other business commitments you must honor in order to continue the use of the company as a customer reference. The revenue is large, but sometimes so are the headaches.

This is usually not the case with midmarket and small and medium business (SMB) customers.

Midmarket and SMB entities range in size between one hundred and 2,500 employees. This market is extremely attractive to businesses for a variety of reasons. First and foremost, these transactions typically have fewer customer executives involved with the decision process, and this leads to shorter sell cycles. This leads to higher deal velocity (more transactions per sales representative) than with enterprise customer engagements. There are fewer requirements from these customers for new product functionality requests or investments in local support. The profit margins are typically higher for these transactions since there is not the involvement of a purchasing department that is measured on the success of their negotiation skills to secure the deepest discount from their vendors.

The smallest segment of the market is small office / home office, which are typically customers with one hundred or fewer employees. This segment is difficult to make profitable with any direct or indirect sales resource investments. Transaction sizes are usually very small, and this segment is best served via a channel partner focused on this segment with other products and services or through an online ecommerce capability.

You will see a more detailed example of this target market analysis later in the chapter.

2. Channel Leverage

The goal of any successful channel program is to recruit, enable, and train partners to drive sales of all of your company's products and solutions. It is critical to treat these partners as an extension of your sales organization. That means that there are clear guidelines and rules of engagement so that channel conflict is not an issue with your internal resources and your valued partner network. It is your responsibility to select the right partners for your business and to train and compensate them well but also to hold them accountable for results.

Why is it important to your sales personnel?

Many sales compensation plans provide incentives to work with channel partners in the field. The best sales representatives will have many trained resources selling their company's products within their respective territory. They know that typically their territory is too large for just one individual to successfully capitalize on all the market opportunity available. Depending on the circumstances, a good sales representative can only close four to six transactions in a quarter. What if your pipeline has ten to twelve leads to close during the current quarter? The best sales representatives know that to successfully manage a territory, they need qualified and talented channel partners to maximize the effectiveness of the sales efforts for the quarter.

Every customer seeks a "trusted adviser" who can assist him or her with the sales engagement process. Many business partners (for example, consulting firms and system integrators) have skills and experience that are valued by the prospective customer. Selecting the right partner will increase the probability of the customer selecting your product or service. Each customer has an existing preferred way to buy, and many prefer doing business with a business partner that can provide added value outside the solutions your company offers the market. It is also very impractical to try to reach all the potential customers with only direct sales resources from your company.

What are the fundamentals of a successful partner engagement? The fundamentals include:

- Two-way dialogue and collaboration is required. Over-communicate to your partners as you would to your existing employees.
- Share opportunities with the partner and engage their support. These resources are a valuable extension to your team but remember that they do not work for you. Treat them as fellow employees and share pipeline data with them to identify the best and most qualified resources to pursue the business opportunity.
- Set expectations up front. Let them know it is a privilege to represent your company's solution to the market, and the opportunity to remain a business partner must be earned.

- Always stay at the dance with the person who brought you to the opportunity. In other words, never take a deal direct once a partner is selected and engaged!
- Partnerships require work. Don't expect the partner to do the deal without your help. Support the sales process and help where appropriate.
- Strive to make your partners self-sufficient with selling your products and services. Incent them to achieve this status. A partner who identifies, qualifies, and closes the deal and supports that transaction without any assistance from your company should receive a higher profit margin than the company that is still very dependent on your sales and support resources.
- Every deal needs to be treated as a win for both parties.
- Hold them accountable. The process disciplines to ensure sales predictability that you will learn in this book apply to both internal and external (channel partners) sales resources.

3. Industry Segmentation

Identify the industries that have the greatest propensity to buy your products and services and align your sales resources accordingly. For example, if your products were associated with the financial services industry, then it would make sense to allocate sales personnel where the industry has a high concentration of companies. New York City would be a location for the financial services industry. Your can assess the number of companies within a targeted industry by using standard industrial classification (SIC) codes.

Map the number of required sales resources to the number of targeted, industry-specific companies that are potential prospective customers for your company. Direct field sales resources are the most expensive sales skills in the industry. It is important that you do your homework and analyze where these resources should be allocated to maximize their contributions to your business.

4. User Experience of Your Products

If your products and services are so intuitive to use and the value is easy to recognize, then this could open many other channels to sell your products to the market without the need for expensive sales resources. Companies like Box (box. com) provide millions of users with secure cloud content management and collaboration. Their platform "allows personal and commercial content to be accessible, sharable, and storable in any format from anywhere." It is very easy to use, and the value is clear. Vast sales resources are not necessary to penetrate large-enterprise customers.

A great example is a company called SolarWinds that develops software for IT management. SolarWinds' products are used by millions of network engineers to manage IT environments ranging from ten to tens of thousands of network devices. Their business model makes the company unique. The company offers a portfolio of free, production-grade network products that engineers can download and use immediately. Although these products are free, they provide significant customer value. The company makes money by offering an upgrade path to fee-based solutions that provide more robust capabilities. In essence, their free products are so effective that the download process is the premier demand generation engine for their sales team. Through this model, the company has penetrated both SMB as well as large-enterprise customers. This is the epitome of a *land and expand* sales model with a very effective use of sales resources due to the user experience of their solutions.

5. Business Model

I have experienced three distinct business models in my career. The first model is *business to business* (B2B) where your company sells directly to another business and your solution is designed to impact the success of that business. An example of this type of business model is Workday. This company has developed HR solutions that are sold directly to other companies to improve their HR efficiency. The second model is *business to consumer* (B2C) where a company sells its product directly to the end consumer. An example of this scenario is Amazon, which sells a variety of consumer products directly to end customers via the web. The third model is *business to business to consumer* (B2B2C) where a company embeds its solution with another company's products. The company bundles a total solution (multiple products from multiple vendors) to its end customers.

The key point of the business model discussion is that the further the end customer (as defined by the person making the purchase decision) is from your business, the more difficult it is to predict business results. In the B2B2C scenario, you are most likely dependent on the sales and marketing efforts of another company to sell your products. Being a layer removed from the end customer impedes your visibility. This is the business model that has the greatest sales predictability challenges.

Putting It All Together

After gathering all this content, you can begin to map out your go-to-market strategy for your company. It is important to address all aspects of your targeted industry with the most cost-effective sales resources.

Look deep into the targeted market segments you feel give your company the greatest opportunity for success. Understand clearly the challenges and risks associated with your desire to enter certain markets. Research is sometimes critical to better understand what it will take to be successful in certain markets. For example, make sure you understand the following issues before investing in a go-to-market strategy:

- What industry segments have the highest propensity to buy your company's products by both vertical (industry: financial services) and horizontal business sectors (cross-industry)?
- What is the total addressable market opportunity available to your company?
- What can we learn from your top revenue-producing customers? Are these repeatable solutions?
- How many enterprise customer targets by size are associated with these vertical markets?
- What are the business drivers and industry dynamics that affect (both positively and negatively) the demand for your company's products in this target segment?
- Who is the economic buyer of your products within this segment? What are the roles and responsibilities of this position? How is the economic buyer measured?

- Who is successful in this market (competition) and why? What are the most significant competitive threats in this industry? Are there barriers to entry? What are the short-term and long-term risks?
- What are the salient characteristics of their solution offering (competition) that contributes to their success in this target vertical (both product and program offerings)?
- What can your company learn from your competitors' strategies within this vertical or target market?
- What is their go-to-market strategy? How many sales resources are dedicated to this market segment? Where are they located? What are the specific roles and responsibilities of these personnel? How much is spent on marketing?
- How well positioned from a product perspective is your company today to successfully enter this market?
- What investments are needed to build a competitive solution offering? Does it require product development or packaging/pricing/positioning of existing solution technology to enter target markets?

A great deal of money can be wasted pursuing market opportunities that really are not appropriate for your company. Learn from your competitions' successes and failures within the targeted segment. If they failed, what makes you think you can succeed? Did they have the right product or service that was in demand by the economic buyer of this segment? Did they have the right skills and expertise from a sales perspective to become a trusted adviser to the top prospective customers in this segment? Has your competition become so entrenched with your prospective customers that there is no short-term opportunity to compete with the incumbent vendor or supplier?

It is imperative that you understand the risks of entering a market. Too often companies get enamored with the large total addressable market opportunity that a company can potentially capitalize on, only to find out their products and services lack required capability to be successful.

After completing a detailed market segmentation study, you can decide to enter a market where you are convinced your company's products and services will be successful. You want to pursue business opportunities within this market segment with the most effective cost of sales labor to grow profitable revenue.

Imagine, for example, that you have identified the financial services industry as having the highest propensity to buy your products and services. You can see that, according to US Census Bureau information, the financial market has over 450,000 entities in the United States to offer your products and services. The challenge is to determine the most effective sales resources to pursue each segment of the market.

These are decisions a sales executive must make in order to build an effective and efficient sales organization. Make the correct decisions, and you will have a highly productive organization that achieves revenue objectives with an appropriate cost of labor. Make bad decisions, and your labor costs will be overwhelming in comparison to the revenue results produce.

Here is an example that highlights the effective use of sales personnel in a multi-channel sales model:

Multi-Channel Go-To-Market Strategy: Financial Services

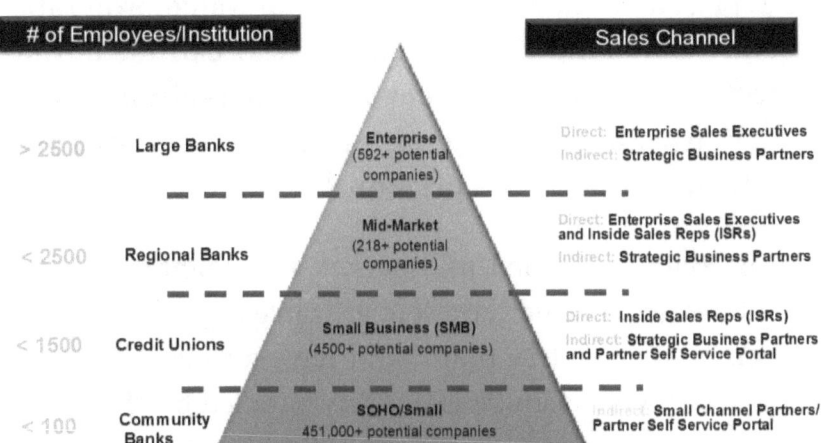

In the above example, cost-effective sales personnel are addressing every segment of the market in a very efficient go-to-market plan. Small community banks can best represent the segment entitled small office / home office (SOHO) with less than one hundred employees. Local business partners can pursue this opportunity or a web-based ecommerce engine or partner portal that enables frictionless and cost-effective customer acquisition capability. This is also where a quality user experience associated with your product can grow revenues without a great deal of manual intervention from a sales labor workforce.

The next segment is small and medium business (SMB) represented by larger credit unions where there are fewer than 1,500 employees within their organization. These are significant-sized businesses that could lead to a larger transaction or long-term business relationship with your company. It is important that you address these opportunities accordingly through trusted partners or your company's inside sales representatives well versed on your value proposition. These are outbound sales resources who call on business prospects within this segment and can typically close a transaction without getting on a plane or leveraging more expensive direct field sales personnel.

The next segment, called midmarket, is a slight variation of the SMB sector. It could represent a sizable regional bank with 2,500 employees or less that could have a more challenging sales process, which can be effectively handled by phone sales. Here I typically see partnership opportunities with both inside sales resources and direct sales personnel. Commission would be split based on who provided the greatest labor to close the transaction. I would also be willing to split 125 percent commission payment when the teamwork was exemplary.

The last segment is represented by large enterprises. The financial entities here are typically the top Fortune 100 banking institutions that require local sales employees to build a relationship with these companies. Sell cycles are longer and more complex, but the transactions are larger to justify the additional cost of sales expense. Channel partners can be a huge influence on the customer's buying process and could be a valuable partner for your company in this sector.

Putting it all together can be complex, but getting it right can make the difference in the success or failure of your go-to-market strategy. Each segment should also be evaluated differently in regard to forecast accuracy. For example, it does not make sense to manage and scrutinize every transaction from the SOHO market since average deal sizes are so small. You will also find later in this book that the process to manage forecast accuracy within the SMB sector (inside sales business model) is very different than that for large enterprise accounts (field sales).

CHAPTER 3

SALES STAGE AND PROCESS DISCIPLINES

Focus on opportunities rather than problems. Problem solving prevents damage, but exploiting opportunities produce results. Unless there is a true crisis, problems shouldn't even be discussed at management meetings until opportunities have been analyzed and dealt with. Exploit change as an opportunity; don't view it as a threat.

—Peter Drucker

One of the most important steps to maximizing the sales predictability and forecast accuracy of your teams is to clearly define every stage of the sales engagement process. This is not a trivial exercise, and both management and field personnel should be involved in defining each sales stage. Every company has different nuances associated with its sell cycles. So what might be tailored for one company may not work for another.

Each stage needs clarity regarding the characteristics and defining milestones associated with that step in the selling process. What are the key prospective client behaviors desired at each stage and what are the process requirements and best practices? What sales tools can be deployed to assist the sales team in accelerating a sales engagement through the selling process?

Each sales stage needs to be clearly defined and structured. This effort ensures that all transactions in the pipeline will be evaluated under the same criteria. Transactions from the pipeline will progress through the sales engagement process in an orderly and well-defined manner. This effort is a key step in sales predictability. The more your sales personnel understand the key milestones required to move a deal through a well-defined sales process, the higher the probability of attaining forecast accuracy.

Ensure your sales stage analysis defines it from your prospective client's perspective. It should reflect your prospective client's buying behavior and expectations. If your sales stages do not reflect your prospective client's point of view, this disconnect can lead to a lost transaction that was in the committed forecast. Your team felt they could not lose the deal when in fact their prospective client felt more comfortable with a competitor who understood their requirements better.

For the XYZ Company, we have identified the following sales stages as an example for this chapter.

Details on each sales stage are as follows:

Sales Stage 1: Identify Prospect

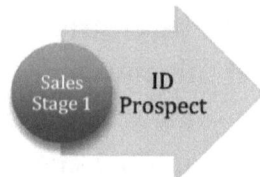

Description: Sales will work with the lead generation team from marketing to jointly prioritize a list of target accounts to begin prospecting activities.

Customer End State: Our company has validated that the prospective client has a sincere interest in learning more about our solution. The prospective client has a clearly defined need, a budget allocated, and an economic buyer identified (decision maker).

Best Practices:

- Sales validates that the prospective client matches the ideal customer profile (target market).
- Understand the historical wins/losses within this industry sector. Establish initial reference list for validation of our company's business value.
- Initiate prospective client contact and begin sales engagement process.
- Align your messaging with the prospective client's economic buyer pain points and assess quality of the sales lead.
- Develop initial mapping of decision maker's role in the decision-making process (build opportunity plan—reference chapter 9 for example).

Process Requirements:

- Create account contacts/opportunity in the SFA/CRM system.
- Update territory plan.
- Build opportunity plan.

Sales Stage 2: Qualify Initial Vision Alignment

Description: The sales representative will have dialogue or meet with the prospective client to determine their business priorities, needs, and business drivers. From this analysis, the sales representative can evaluate the potential fit of the company's solution and mutually assess the sales engagement process milestones. A key step is to identify the economic sponsor who typically

- owns the business problem, holds the budget, and is empowered to allocate funding for your solution;
- has the necessary authority to drive the prospective client's buying process;
- will influence the other influencers and decision makers for recommendations; and
- can deploy the resources and funds to implement the project.

Customer End State: Our company has a good understanding of the business challenges of the prospective client. We will engage the prospective client on a deeper needs analysis and solution development endeavors. The economic sponsor will drive this initiative.

Best Practices:

- Bring thought leadership as you test the prospective client's problems, existing infrastructure, and higher-level business and technical objectives.
- Identify and address the prospective client's concerns and risks associated with your proposed solution alternative.
- Use industry-relevant customer examples to gain alignment, present new ideas, and show knowledge of customer business.
- Leverage all potential contacts within the prospective client to uncover business, political, technical, and personal influences affecting the decision process.
- Proactively identify competitive threats under consideration and their influence on the prospective client 's vision.
- Be willing to qualify out and drop the pursuit of the business. Don't waste valuable funding and resources pursing a business opportunity that most likely will not result in a sale for your company.

Process Requirements:

- Update opportunity plan.

Sales Stage 3: Identify Business Needs and Requirements

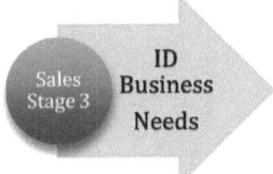

Description: The sales representative coordinates a series of meetings with the prospective client's executives and appropriate company resources to understand the business problems/pain, technical requirements, and other factors related to the decision-making process. Evaluation events may include responses to RFIs, RFPs, and other technical documentation.

Customer End State: The company has a good solution that will meet the prospective client's needs. The prospective client likes our initial recommendations and is collaboratively engaged in solution development with our company.

Best Practices:

- Identify the key metrics (business and technical) critical to the economic sponsor. It is also important to understand the cost of implementing your solution versus either remaining with the existing solution or delaying or canceling the project.
- Ensure you identify each stakeholder and their personal and business agendas in the decision process.
- Ensure a thorough understanding of currently installed solutions, prospective client's architectural requirements, and overall philosophies affecting the decision process.

Process Requirements:

- Update account contacts/opportunity in the SFA/CRM system.
- Update opportunity plan.

Sales Stage 4: Confirm Buying Process

Description: The sales representative identifies the prospective client's typical buying process and aligns with the executive sponsor on the needed steps and involved parties with each sales milestone (e.g., technical evaluation, proof of concept, legal negotiations, and procurement disciplines). This includes preliminary budget alignment, approval process, and procurement process as well as desired implementation time frame. The sales team understands how funding will be secured and who is ultimately responsible for the success of the initiative.

Customer End State: The prospective client has agreed with the company on a process to evaluate their proposed solution and has clearly communicated the decision criteria that will be used in the decision-making process.

Best Practices:

- Identify their entire decision and approval process, including all potentially involved parties and their roles in the decision process.
- Identify what alternatives the prospective client is evaluating and who is involved with this analysis.
- Independently confirm your understanding of the buying process with at least three prospective client contacts.
- Document the prospective client buying process, showing each step ands involved parties.
- Anticipate potential hidden steps or required approvals (CFO, IT Steering or Architectural Committee) and include them in your plan.
- Identify specifics on how the project will be funded and who owns the associated budget.
- The decision criteria that the prospective client will use in the buying process are clearly understood, and the probability of the company winning the business is very good.
- Be willing to qualify out of the business opportunity if it is not a good fit or the deal closing does not appear likely.

Process Requirements:

- Update account contacts/opportunity in the SFA/CRM system.
- Update opportunity plan.

Sales Stage 5: Determine Solution

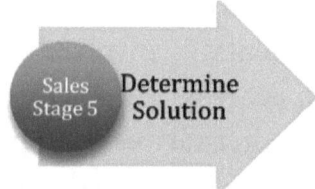

Description: The sales representative coordinates all activities during the multiple meetings with the executive sponsor and other executives instrumental to the decision process of the prospective client. The sales representative has documented a formal business case highlighting the business value for the prospective client and is within known constraints (budget, resources, time frame). The sales representative and/or account team presents a proposal (business and technical) and gains prospective client agreement to proceed with a proof of concept, trial, or a decision to buy the proposed solution.

Customer End State: The company has proven to all prospective client stakeholders that the proposed solution is the best alternative for their business requirements.

Best Practices:

- Use a consultative approach, focused on their highest-order business needs, to guide the prospective client to a decision for the proposed solution.
- Only demonstrate capability that is linked to specific, known needs to avoid stalling the decision.
- Communicate and demonstrate a tight linkage between your solution and the executive sponsor's critical requirements.

- Use case studies and references that prove the capability to deliver the proposed business value.
- Fully understand the strengths ands weaknesses of your proposed solution in comparison to your competition.

Process Requirements:

- Deliver a clear and concise proposal.
- If trial is required, create and deliver the results as they pertain to the trail success criteria.
- Update opportunity in the SFA/CRM system.
- Update opportunity plan.
- To ensure accurate forecasting, use the Opportunity Qualification Checklist.

Sales Stage 6: Present Solution

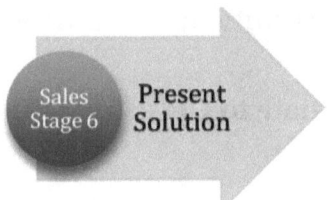

Description: The sales representative and/or account team provides a formal proposal that tailors the business value of the proposed solution to the specific problem areas of the prospective client. Business benefits should be quantified to ensure the prospective client acknowledges financial justification.

Customer End State: The prospective client has received the proposal from the vendor, and the benefits of the proposed solution are clearly defined and recognized by our executive team.

Best Practices:

- Document in the proposal a clear understanding of the prospective client's pain point and business and technical requirements.
- Present financial justification that shows an indisputable reason to buy the proposed solution.
- Highlight an effective and efficient implementation plan that accelerates the time to benefit from the proposed solution.
- If necessary, show product road map commitments that demonstrate the commitment to protect the prospective client's investment with the proposed solution via future product enhancements.

Process Requirements:

- Update opportunity in the SFA/CRM system.

Sales Stage 7: Negotiate to Close

Description: The sales representative and/or account team proactively manages the process with the prospective client's legal, finance, and order management teams to ensure the decision timeline progresses as agreed to by both parties. Pricing, payment, and legal terms are confirmed, and the prospective client becomes a customer by signing the final contracts and in some cases issues a purchase order.

Customer End State: The customer has selected the proposed solution, and has initiated the procurement process.

Best Practices:

- Determine last-minute objections and potential deal breakers and address early.
- Leverage the executive team from your company to establish corporate commitment if necessary.
- Identify at-risk stakeholders and engage with appropriate resources.
- When available, build rapport with the prospective client's procurement and legal personnel involved with the final stages of the procurement process.
- Directly engage all decision makers rather than relying on prospective client staff personnel to internally sell your solution.

Process Requirements:

- Update opportunity in the SFA/CRM system.

Defining each of these steps is a critical task in establishing a framework for forecast accuracy. All sales engagements need to be managed on a consistent basis. Each member of your team must have a clear understanding of each sales stage as it pertains to each revenue opportunity. This includes all sales and marketing resources.

CHAPTER 4

MARKETING OPERATION METRICS

No matter how brilliant your mind or strategy, if your playing a solo game, you'll always lose out to a team.
—Reid Hoffman, LinkedIn cofounder

The relationship between sales and marketing can differ dramatically from company to company. The best have sales and marketing leadership that collaborate on all decisions and share equally in the success or failure of their efforts. The worst have leadership styles where credit for success is single-minded and blame for failures lead to finger pointing and resentment. I have seen it all. The team that collaborates will have more success. It also leads to a culture that encourages teamwork and joint execution.

The best companies recognize that sales are very dependent on marketing and marketing can't recognize success without sales. Assessing the analytic interlock between sales and marketing can provide the necessary visibility that could be the difference between success and failure. Marketing traditionally has ownership and the responsibility to nurture the prospects before sales gets involved. This is a very important requirement for any transactional or sales engagement success.

New trends in marketing analytics have increased the visibility and accountability associated with marketing leadership and its contribution to the revenue success of the company. This was not always the case in past years. The poor marketing organizations view revenue growth as a sales function and see marketing as only a support role or a simple cost center. Accountability for results is unwanted and avoided at all cost. To be successful, marketing leadership must embrace this responsibility. The best marketing leaders are confident in their contributions to the business. They want the spotlight on the impact that the marketing organization has on the revenue growth of the company. They work closely with sales and share equally in their mutual success.

Marketing is instrumental in creating great value for a company, and today's CEOs recognize that investments with marketing programs and campaigns can greatly impact the revenue and profit success of the company. Today's innovative CEOs can use the same marketing analytics to assess the true ROI of the marketing organization. Success can lead to increased funding for the best performing and most efficient marketing organizations.

Everyone has heard the old adage that nothing happens without a sale. This is true but also overstated. The entire sales process that leads to revenue recognition starts with marketing. This is why having visibility into the effectiveness of the marketing pipeline is as important as visibility into the efficiency of the sales cycle. It requires establishing goals and objectives that are achievable. There is a healthy understanding that program and campaign investments are significant enough to reach the established goals and that the organization is staffed to succeed.

These marketing investments must start with the expected committed outcome as measured by revenue and profit. This is difficult if not impossible without clear understanding of the ROI associated with each dollar of marketing investment. This process starts with clear, measurable metrics with targets critical to the desired success of the company. I have never met a CFO who would not increase marketing investment when there was high confidence that the ROI of that investment would be recognized.

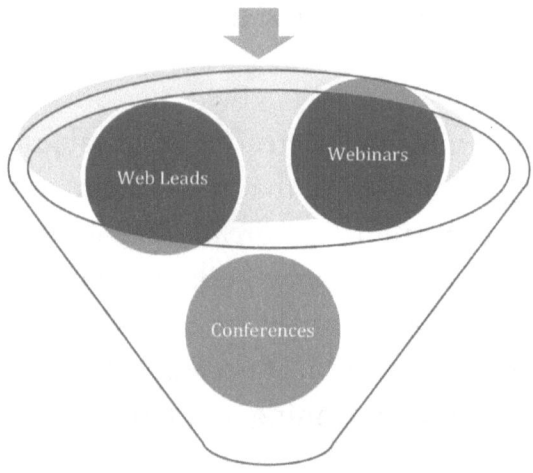

Not all marketing investments can be directly tied to revenue and profits. For example, conference and webinar attendance will lead to soft goals such as participation metrics. These metrics are important, but the closer a marketing executive can tie these measurements to revenue and profit, the more credibility will be earned by the marketing organization.

Measuring the ROI of any marketing organization must include all associated costs. These include campaign development and deployment, media expenses, direct marketing, brand investments, advertising and marketing staff (full-time and contractor expenses). It is imperative to avoid showing erroneous returns on marketing investments to senior leadership. Any financial justification must include all associated costs. Failure to do so is the fastest way to lose credibility with your company's CFO.

Throughout this chapter, you will learn about numerous marketing key performance indicators that will help your efforts to predict sales. It is important to pick metrics and the timing of the measurements that are most relevant to your business. You don't have to measure everything. Less is more. Make sure all your measurements focus on results, not just marketing-based activities. Decide the most important marketing measurements to your success and incorporate assessment into your daily routine. Remember—what gets measured gets done.

These measurements must all lead to decisions. Why would you measure anything that can't lead to a decision that will help marketing effectiveness and efficiency? For example, a conference that produces numerous leads that none turned into revenue begs the question regarding the value of that conference investment. Maybe the attendees were not executive sponsors for your solution or were not empowered to decide on your behalf. You have to question why you would invest in this marketing expense in future years when other conferences yielded better results. The best and most well-organized marketing investments are worthless if they don't produce revenue and profit results. Trust me that your CFO will not care about your success with any marketing metric if it doesn't contribute directly to the revenue and profit success of the company. You must constantly ask yourself, "What is the best way to invest my marketing budget that will yield the greatest revenue and profit results for the company?"

Sales metrics are measured throughout each stage of the sales cycle. Most sales engagement cycles start with a qualified lead and end with contract and solution deployment. But more often than not, marketing through buyer awareness starts the revenue cycle before sales gets involved. Each stage must be agreed to by sales and marketing. This includes agreement on terminology. For example, what is the definition of a lead? Is it really just a prospect until it gets qualified? What then is a qualified lead? I have seen these issues lead to heated debates between sales and marketing leadership. This process may be painful, but it is critically necessary to clearly understand the contributions from marketing and to ensure all measurements are accurate.

Sales cycles are identified in later chapters of this book and should be measured on an ongoing basis. Traditionally, marketing did not go through this same methodology or scrutiny with regard to the revenue cycle of a company. That is no longer the case. Marketing organizations today have the same scrutiny as sales organizations in both prosperous times and challenging times. Both sales and marketing must own their respected contributions to predictable, profitable revenue growth.

Before we discuss the key performance indicators that should be measured within the marketing organization, we need to address the pipeline funnel that will be instrumental to assess the impact of marketing on a company. It is also crucially important that each stage of the revenue cycle is clearly defined in regard to roles and responsibilities among marketing and sales teams.

This includes a smooth and uneventful transition of responsibilities from marketing to sales. For example, do sales personnel have any role or responsibility with lead development or nurturing? Who does lead qualification? These discussions have led to the emergence of a hybrid role between marketing and sales called *lead development rep*, whose sole responsibility is to qualify a lead before it goes to sales.

Another example is measurement. Who will measure the effectiveness and efficiency of the marketing organization? Will it be sales operations? Finance? Who sets the targets for the marketing organization? Are these measurements agreed to by sales? Both marketing and sales leadership can avoid headaches when each stage of the revenue cycle has clearly defined metrics as well as role and responsibility clarity.

Below is an example of a revenue cycle for a company. Please note that your specific revenue cycle should reflect the specifics of your company. You might have more or fewer stages. The most important thing is to ensure it is tailored to your business.

Marketing is typically responsible for the first three stages of the revenue cycle as highlighted with the above chart. We will discuss the details of the sales stages later in the book. Let's break down the first three stages before we explore proper marketing metrics.

Inquires: This is the first stage of the funnel and can include any source of business, such as webinar participants, direct mailing lists, and conference event attendees. This is where the marketing efforts in many companies start. It could be as simple as a mailing list purchased for all CFOs (if this executive is a typical buyer of your solution) within a specific industry. Key metrics to track are as follows:

- How much is your company paying for inquiries?
- What is the conversion success from inquiry to prospect? What percentage eventually close?
- What percentage of the inquiries turn into prospects? (Goal should be between 35 and 45 percent.)

Prospect: These are executives who have engaged the company and have expressed interest in your solution or service offering. It could be a webinar attendee who has asked for a follow-up meeting with sales. It could be a web contact where a free whitepaper was requested and downloaded. We know they might have interest in our solution offerings but not enough to pass it to sales. Key metrics to track are as follows:

- What percentage of prospects converts to qualified leads? (Goal should be between 20 and 30 percent.)
- What percentage eventually close?

Qualified Lead: This is where a contact from marketing or a lead development rep contacts the potential customer to assess the real potential opportunity for the company. Lead development reps are far more cost efficient than passing prospects over to sales for the qualification stage. Before sales gets engaged, marketing assesses if this is a qualified lead by determining the following:

- Is the prospect also the decision maker for our product or solution? Is the prospect an influencer to the decision? Who will ultimately make the decision on behalf of our solution offering, and will we be granted access to this executive?
- What are the problems the customer is trying to solve, and how good a fit is our solution?
- Is this a company that typically buys our company's solution offering?
- Is there budget allocated for our company's solution offering?
- When will a decision be made for our company's solution offering?
- What is the buying cycle of the prospect, and what stage are they at today?
- What competition is also being evaluated?

Lead qualification questions can be scored so that they can be prioritized to sales. Top opportunities should be treated with a higher sense of urgency. You can also introduce SLA metrics (service level agreements) that can define the actual time frame each stage of the revenue cycle must be completed by before moving to the next stage. For example, all web leads must be contacted within four business hours. Sales must respond to all qualified leads within twenty-four hours. This discipline can greatly enhance the acceleration of an opportunity through the revenue cycle.

You can use the same metrics as the first two stages:

- What percentage of qualified leads convert to sales opportunities? (Goal should be between 7 and 10 percent.)
- What percentage eventually close?

Marketing metrics can fall into multiple categories. Again, measure what is most critical to your business and don't measure anything that can't lead to a decision that will help grow revenues and profits. These categories are as follows:

Revenue Key Performance Indicators

Marketing's contribution to the revenue and profit success of the company needs to be clearly understood by all senior leadership, especially the chief financial officer. Why this is important is that the CFO only cares about metrics that contribute to shareholder value. Any metric that can show where an increased investment could yield growth in revenue, profit margin, or cash flow will catch the CFO's attention. For example, these five KPIs are usually assessed on a regular basis:

- **Percentage of Pipeline Deals Sourced from Marketing:** In most companies, the percentage of deals sourced from marketing to sales should be approximately 60 percent of the overall pipeline. This metric is typically derived from trend analysis (past marketing performance) and agreed to early in the year by both marketing and sales leadership. Again, this should be evaluated on a regular basis, and trending should also be monitored. This measurement is a quantity versus quality issue.
- **Percentage of Pipeline Revenue Sourced from Marketing:** Similar to the previous KPI, percentage

of revenue is also important to track. For example, marketing can be successful in achieving its percentage of pipeline deals, but if the revenue falls short of the 60 percent target that is an indication that the deals sourced from marketing are smaller than what is required. This measurement is a quantity versus quality issue as well.

- **Win Percentage from Transactions Sourced from Marketing:** This measurement assesses the quality of the deals sourced from marketing. Again, if marketing sources 60 percent of the pipeline but the win rate is below target, this could represent that the leads were not accurately qualified.

- **Marketing Investment per Pipeline Stage:** How much should marketing spend for an inquiry, prospect, or qualified lead? Are these costs trending up or down? Why is there variance to this trending?

- **Marketing Expense as a Percentage of Revenue:** This is the ultimate measurement and one that the CFO will assess on a regular basis. This should include total marketing expenses, including all program spending, advertising, and all personnel costs. The CFO will check on a quarterly basis the trends on this expense item and how it pertains to marketing's contribution to overall revenue. It is common to assess this measurement by including sales expense as well. Percentages of this KPI will change based on industry dynamics as well as business models. If the company's solution portfolio is complex and requires significant field resources, the percentage of sales and marketing spending will differ dramatically from a consumer product that can be sold exclusively through the web.

Marketing Effectiveness and Efficiency

Marketing effectiveness and efficiency is about how well marketing dollars are spent to achieve the goals and objectives of the organization. This is important to show the incremental contributions for each marketing investment. These metrics are typically for the marketing leadership, but the CFO will want to know what is working and what is not so that invest/divest decisions can be made to grow the company. For example:

- **Lead Generation by Program Spending:** Marketing spends marketing dollars to generate revenue. Some program investments are proven performers, whereas others can be more experimental. It is imperative that marketing leadership knows what investments are working and what areas of the budget should be redirected to more profitable initiatives. Assess the conversion rate of each program spending in order to prioritize your marketing budget.
- **Cost per Lead:** What is the marketing cost for each qualified lead? Is it trending in a positive direction, which would mean you are working smarter with your marketing investments? This measurement should be assessed for each marketing channel.
- **Cost of Customer Acquisition (CAC):** The cost of acquisition can be calculated by simply dividing all the costs spent on acquiring more customers (marketing expenses) by the number of customers acquired in the period the money was spent. Put another way, it is the cost to convince a prospective customer to purchase your product or service. If it cost your company $100,000 to generate 1,000 customers, then your CAC measurement

is a hundred dollars per new customer. Knowing the CAC for each marketing channel is a critical measurement for marketing leadership.

- **Marketing Velocity:** Marketing velocity is the speed or rate at which marketing efforts yield business results. In simple terms, this is how fast you take a customer from interest to purchase. Velocity is about doing things faster, and marketing velocity can be accelerated through the use of marketing automation, CRM, and other tools. This measurement is critical for marketing organizations to learn how effective their marketing collateral, tactics, and strategies are at producing business results. The number of leads that move into each stage is the first step to generating a velocity assessment.

Web Effectiveness and Predictability

Marketing analytics can provide a direct link between marketing investments and business results. Web analytics are metrics that typically only the marketing organization cares about since it measures the effectiveness of your website. These measurements are usually not presented to C-level executives since most do not care about page load times, bounce rates, page views per visit, time duration on site, download statistics, and visitor loyalty analysis. With web analytics, the metric analysis must lead to conclusions regarding reader intention.

Marketing executives can get caught up in information overload and not come to any conclusions or decisions based on the mountain of data that is analyzed. The number of page views or visitors to your website mean nothing if it does not connect with meaningful key performance indicators that predict revenue.

As with any marketing investment (campaigns, programs, web events), set up conversion goals for each investment and monitor accordingly.

- **Web Leads—Pay-per-Click Statistics:** The pay-per-click measurement is associated with ads or advertisements on a website to attract new customers. How it works is every time your ad is clicked, sending a visitor to your website, you pay the search engine a small fee. It is important to assess if you are recognizing the appropriate ROI for this marketing investment.
- **Qualified Leads Gained through Website:** This measurement highlights the effectiveness of your web page to generate leads. This can measure the download rate of a new whitepaper or eBook that can be a lead generation engine for your company. This will also be a reflection of the quality and effectiveness of your marketing collateral.
- **Web Content Conversion to Revenue:** All web-marketing investments should be evaluated and assessed by only one criteria—and that is how well they convert a prospect to revenue.

Customer Satisfaction and Loyalty

Customer satisfaction and loyalty is about marketing's contribution to the customer experience with your product or service. For example:

- **Net Promoter Score:** According to Wikipedia, a net promoter or net promoter score (NPS) is a management tool that can be used to gauge the loyalty of a firm's customer relationships. It serves as an alternative to traditional customer satisfaction research and claims to be correlated with revenue growth.

The measurement of this KPI is fairly simple. Your customers are asked on a scale of one to ten how satisfied they are with the products and service offerings. If a customer scores your company a nine or ten, that customer is considered a *loyal enthusiast* and is willing to recommend your company's products or services to others. If your customers score your company a seven or eight, they are considered *passively satisfied*. They are not loyal to your company and are willing to try your competition when offered. A score of seven or lower dictates that these customers are *detractors* or unhappy customers. They have had a poor experience with your company and are not willing to recommend your products and services.

- **Customer Retention:** This measurement is to assess how successful your company is in retaining its customers. *Churn rate* is the percentage of customers who end their relationship with a company in a given period. It typically is presented as a percentage of the customer base that renews for your company. In many public companies, this is a very important metric that Wall Street uses to evaluate the success a company has with customer satisfaction. Success with this metric can be a growth factor in shareholder value.

Companies with high retention rates are doing something very right for their customers. It is a reflection of the value generated from your products or services but also how easy it is to do business with your company, which includes the impact your customer support organization has on client satisfaction. This measurement is also reflected as a *churn ratio* that is the inverse of your customer retention rate. Obviously, high churn rates need to be evaluated for root cause analysis to determine why certain customers do not renew their business relationship with your company.

If your company utilizes a free product offering as a demand generation tool, such as a free app, it is extremely important to assess the *free-to-paid conversion rate*. This model is typically associated with software companies that offer a freemium solution with an upgrade path to a full-function paid upgrade.

Another subset of customer retention is to determine your company's overall *customer retention costs* (CRC). This is a measurement to determine how much investment in sales, marketing, and customer support is required to keep your customers satisfied and retained.

- **Lifetime Value (LTV):** This measurement is simply the value of your customer over a lifetime. It highlights the importance of customer retention's impact on current and future revenue. Lose a customer, and it impacts immediate revenue contributions but also revenue over time. This metric is the total revenue contributed by a customer over the time of the relationship with that customer.

It is a complex calculation made up of many variables and can be calculated in different ways. The most common calculation associated with LTV is average monthly revenue per customer multiplied by the gross margin per customer. This number is the average monthly profit per customer. That figure is then divided by the monthly churn rate.

Another variation of LTV calculation is more focused on retention and is a little more complex. The calculation here consists of the following steps:

1. Determine the average customer lifespan, which is the time duration a typical customer lasts with your company.
2. Determine what will be the revenue generated by this customer over the life of the relationship. This includes current revenue and future upgrades and new product acquisitions.
3. Assess the costs of delivering your products and services.
4. Then assess the net present value (NPV) of these future amounts. NPV is the difference between the present value of cash inflows and the present value of cash outflows.

Obviously, the higher your customer's satisfaction with your products and services, the greater the value associated with your lifetime value calculations. It is a critical measurement since it highlights the financial impact and value that is associated with repeat business. The greatest leverage a company can have with their LTV measurement is outstanding customer service. Healthy companies do a recurring self-evaluation of their customer experience from onboarding a new customer to ongoing support. If this customer experience is instrumental in building customer loyalty, it will be reflected in positive growth of your LTV measurement.

CHAPTER 5

INSIDE SALES METRICS

Expect what you inspect.
—Edward Deming, the father of
Total Quality Management

Inside sales has been referred to as remote sales, call center sales, or virtual sales. Most commonly, use of the term *inside sales* refers to leveraging phone sale expertise to sell your products or services, typically to small and medium businesses. Direct sales, also referred to as field sales, are associated with a more complex sales engagement. This complexity requires face-to-face interaction. Inside sales continues to be a rapidly growing sales investment area due to the low cost of sales associated with this sales channel. Reduced travel requirements and lower infrastructure costs contribute to the attractiveness of this sales investment.

In the past, inside sales was only used to generate leads for the more experienced and well-trained field sales personnel. This philosophy has dramatically changed in recent years. Early-stage companies have leveraged the inside sales model to establish market presence and then invest later in field sales personnel to pursue larger, enterprise-sized customers. This is typically where the product or service is very complex and the targeted customers require more personal interactions with sales resources.

Inside sales also were viewed as a high-velocity sales channel where closing deals quickly and efficiently were valued versus the longer sell cycles associated with field sales personnel. The belief was that inside sales required less training and experience than field sales personnel. Nothing could be further from the truth.

As more companies increase their sales investment toward the inside sales model, these same companies are also committing more resources to ensuring the skills and expertise of their inside sales team rival those of their field sales counterparts. This is why many of the same measurements we hold field sales accountable for can also be applied to the inside sales team.

Inside sales talent and expertise is valued now more than ever before. This skill set is in demand by companies both large and small. With the advances in technology and sales tools available today, such as webinar conferences and online trials, the ability to reach multiple prospective clients remotely has never been easier.

In recent years, we have seen a migration from field sales where the cost of labor is very expensive to inside sales where the ROI is more attractive. A decision for an inside sales model is also predicated on a number of factors, such as the following:

- What is the complexity of the product or service you are selling?
- What is the total contract value (TCV) of your products or services? Total contract value is a metric that

represents the value of one-time and recurring charges. It does not include usage charges. High TCV typically requires field sales personnel to be involved with the sales engagement.

- Who is the economic buyer of your solution? If it requires senior decision authority, that may dictate field sales personnel.
- What is the length of the sales engagement cycle? Long sell cycles may dictate field sales resources. Typical inside sales models have less than a sixty-day sell cycle.
- What is the size of your typical client? Small or medium-sized businesses are very much associated with an inside sales model.

It is also as important as ever to establish strong performance metrics to manage the inside sales organization. It is imperative that every step in the sales process has appropriate visibility and scrutiny.

Before we discuss sales metrics associated with high-velocity sales models such as inside sales, it is important to note a transformation going on with this business model. The skills and expertise between inside and field sales are getting more aligned. This also leads to a convergence in the metrics used to evaluate performance with these two sales models.

Regardless if your sales model is B2B (business to business where the end customer is a business entity) or B2C (business to consumer where the end customer is a specific person), the inside sale process involves multiple touch points. This can include multiple responsibilities, including sales prospecting, lead qualification (similar to lead development rep), inbound sales response, or responsibility for the entire sales cycle, including the closing and contract activities.

For the purpose of this chapter, we will focus on inside sales personnel who have the responsibility for inbound lead response and closing business directly.

Activity-based sales metrics have traditionally been the methodology to measure inside sales performance. In recent years, these measures, such as call volumes and responsiveness, call duration, meetings and demos scheduled, have become less important since the focus has shifted to more results-oriented goal performance. But these metrics are still used today and provide valuable feedback on inside sales rep performance.

- **Time to Response**

This measures how quickly a rep responds to an inbound lead. It should be very concerning for any company to have a time-to-response metric greater than one day. Most desired targets should be measured in four to six business hours. It could be an e-mail or phone response, but being timely with any lead or inquiry gives a good first impression.

- **Abandonment Rates**

Also important and very much aligned with the time-to-response metric is abandonment rate. This measures the percentage of inbound callers who hang up or disengage before an inside sales rep can address the inquiry. Nothing should be more painful for a company to accept than abandonment rates. You should expect to lose that opportunity and never hear from that prospective customer again.

If you have a high abandonment rate, this will be no secret in the industry. I have known customer support organizations of my competitors with wait times of over one hour. I leveraged this point in competitive engagements by asking prospective customers to call my help desk and to do the same with poorly performing competitors. I won a great deal of business by doing this to my competition. Poor abandonment rates basically push business opportunities to your competition.

- **Call Time per Lead/Inquiry**

Again, these metrics may not be as important as with outbound prospecting, but you want to ensure your inside reps are actively pursuing sales opportunities in a time-effective manner. For example, I have seen measurements with this metric that seek inside sales reps to talk to at least five to seven prospective clients every hour. This will fluctuate based on the complexity of your solution and the size of your target customers.

- **Sales Cycle Duration**

This reflects the velocity aspect typically associated with inside sales. How long does it typically take to close a sale by your inside sales team? The ultimate goal is to close as many customers as possible with realistic productivity metrics while maintaining overall professionalism. You want your prospective customer to view your inside sales team as subject matter experts and trusted advisers, but at the same time, you need to ensure sales engagements don't run forever.

- **Average Order Size by Rep**

What inside sales reps close the largest deals? Why? Any sales organization (inside, direct, or channel) needs to become a "learning organization." This means sharing best practices with the entire sales team. If an inside sales rep typically has a larger order size over time, then what tactics or methodologies can be shared with others to maximize overall productivity?

- **Time Selling Percentage**

Time management is a critical element to managing an inside sales team. How much time does your team spend selling versus other nonrevenue-producing activities? Obviously there are activities that contribute to team productivity, such as sales training and professional education. But how often do your team members get pulled away from their phone responsibilities to attend meetings? Some meetings are important, but it is not good for anyone to have any unproductive time associated with an inside sales team. More than any other sales model, inside sales reps are very much "coin operated" in that the more they work, the more they make. If you have too many nonrevenue activities impacting productivity, the first group to complain will be your inside sales team. It is important to be very sensitive to their time since it is in direct correlation to their earnings.

Performance metrics that apply to both inside sales as well as field sales personnel are covered in later chapters.

CHAPTER 6

CHANNEL SALES METRICS

When I see companies that don't execute, the chances are that they don't measure, don't reward, and don't promote people who know how to get things done.

—Larry Bossidy,
former CEO of Honeywell International

A channel sale is the most understood of all the sales business models. By definition, a channel sale is where the company employs a third party, a reseller to sell their products on to their customers. It has its benefits as well as challenges.

A channel sales business model has enormous upside if managed correctly by the company. By outsourcing the sales function, you have the opportunity to greatly expand your sales capability in a very cost-effective manner. Channel Sales should be viewed as an extension of your internal sales and marketing team and in some ways should be treated as employees. Having an effective channel sales strategy enables the following:

Relationships: Many times, the channel partners have business relationships with the most desired target prospects. Instead of investing years establishing new executive relationships, companies can engage a channel partner who already does business with this prospect.

Customer Experience: Channel partners can have detailed understanding on how potential prospects want to be sold to by a vendor. This experience is invaluable in shortening sell cycles.

Technical Support: In certain circumstances, the channel partner will also provide the technical support, dramatically reducing your cost of sales. It is recommended that any company that also outsources the technical support function ensures that the channel personnel are certified on the technical aspects of your products and services.

New Revenue Opportunities: Through proper training and certification, many channel sales partners can be completely self-sufficient with their sales and marketing programs. Self-sufficient channel partners will dictate a higher commission payment due to their inherent costs that you will no longer incur in your company's cost-of-sales calculations. By being self-sufficient, the channel partner builds your pipeline with little or no labor costs from your company.

Expertise: Channel partners can provide experience that does not exist with your company. For example, your company decides to pursue business with various federal government agencies. Your company has no experience selling to this complex customer segment, nor do you have the contractual certifications required to conduct business with most federal agencies. Using dedicated federal government resellers not only helps open doors with established relationships but also shortens the sell cycle through already existing infrastructure and contractual investments.

Competitive Information: A close channel partner can also be instrumental in providing valuable competitive information.

A channel sales business model does require a significant investment by your company. It is not as simple as just outsourcing the sales function to an external third party. Your company is still responsible for ensuring that third parties do not diminish the customer experience of your product or services. Significant training is required to ensure that any channel partner can clearly and accurately communicate your company's value proposition similar to your internal sales and marketing teams. Although this investment can be significant, a successful channel sales model, if managed correctly, can provide a distribution model that is less costly than expensive internal sales resources.

In regard to forecast accuracy of this business model, you will see many similarities to managing the accountability of your internal sales team. You will see many differences as well. Just like your internal team, channel sales partners and resellers demand strategic clarity with the relationship. They want a clear understanding of what is expected of the relationship. Will a quota be assigned where if numbers are not met, then the relationship is terminated? Is the commission plan easy to understand, and does it incent the right behavior? Will there be any channel conflict with the internal sales team over targeted opportunities? Will there be consistency in your channel programs over time? Are you an easy company to do business with in regard to channel sales?

The better you manage the channel business process disciplines, visibility into your own business operations, and channel sales incentive program, the more success you will recognize with your reseller community. Investments in these areas will provide the strategic clarity necessary for forecast accuracy from partners.

Things go wrong with forecast accuracy when confusion exists in these areas:

Channel conflict exists with internal sales teams. This is almost always the result of vague or poorly defined rules of engagement with the internal sales organization. For example, both the internal sales team and the channel reseller feel they own a certain opportunity to be assigned for them to close. A clear and concise deal registration process is a way to avoid this channel conflict. If your internal team uses Salesforce. com for deal registration, then it should also be mandatory for your channel partners to use the same system. This includes visibility into your pipeline for strategic and trusted partners so they know what opportunities are available and what has been assigned to internal sales resources.

Poorly defined compensation structure. A lack of clarity with the compensation structure for your resellers will derail your channel sales business model. If you are willing to invest the necessary training resources to ensure your channel resellers will be self-sufficient, they should be paid accordingly. Said another way, if your resellers are willing to make the commitment to be self-sufficient (own the demand generation, lead qualification, sell cycle management, close and contract signing), they should be paid more than partners who simply want a company to feed them leads for closure. One partner (Reseller A) sources the opportunity and closes the deal without any assistance from your company. The other partner (Reseller B) is dependent on your team for leads and possibly sales support activities like demos and webinars. Reseller A lowers your cost of sales since your company does not need internal resources to support their sales efforts. They should make a higher commission percentage than Reseller B. This incentive system needs to be clearly communicated and documented to avoid all confusion. If a partner feels that they were not treated fairly from a compensation standpoint, expect them to terminate the relationship and possibly pursue a relationship with your competition.

Lack of channel partner support. Even the best-managed reseller programs still have the need for conflict resolution. Issues will always be escalated to address concerns, such as product functionality enhancement requests, unique support requirements, and pricing and discount demands from reseller business opportunities. Partners will at times ask to partner with internal sales and marketing resources that increase the odds of winning a key opportunity. It is critical that there is a clear escalation path for any issue from your reseller community. They need to know their voice is heard and that your company will be responsive to their challenges. Make sure your internal channel sales team is staffed to succeed. Your channel partners will view this as a clear sign of commitment.

Unrealistic revenue expectations. Just like your internal sales team, they want to ensure their annual targets are challenging but achievable. A reseller will be hesitant to make expensive investments to build an external sales team for your company if they have unrealistic expectations on quota assignments and unacceptable consequences for falling short of expectations. It is recommended to take your most trusted partners and include them in the annual revenue-planning process.

To ensure sales forecast accuracy is maximized with your channel reseller partners, you need to ensure the same process discipline exists with your partners as with your internal sales team. They should all adhere to the same forecast and reporting requirements. This includes commitment from all resellers across the entire revenue engine. Partners need to adhere to how you manage your sales and marketing business processes. Your company's foundation for forecast accuracy should not change or be modified to accommodate any external channel partner. All opportunities in your pipeline and sales stage processes should be managed the same across both internal and external sales resources. Consistency is the key to forecast accuracy with external business partners.

Successful sales leaders hate surprises both good and bad. When a business partner brings in a large opportunity that was not planned or that your company did not forecast, the temptation is to celebrate this good fortune. But the best sales executives want to know why there was no visibility into the deal. They want to know why it was not discussed during formal pipeline reviews. It is imperative that all your channel partners understand that this lack of transactional visibility is not acceptable and will not be tolerated in the future. You would have the same conversation with any internal sales resource who plays this game. Remember that your resellers are an extension of your sales team. They need to be held accountable to that same standard. This is why two CRM systems (one for your internal team and one for resellers) should never be tolerated.

Collaboration is critical to the success of any channel community, especially as it comes to forecast accuracy. Your business partners can produce significant contributions in customer acquisition and revenue growth but only if information flows freely and expectations are clearly set and communicated. This will lead to a channel-centric culture that will pay dividends if managed correctly.

As mentioned earlier, you need to manage the forecast accuracy of your partners the same as your sales team. Many of the metrics referenced earlier in the book can be applied to external sales channel partners. There do exist some metrics that measure the effectiveness and efficiency of your reseller community that your channel management leadership must monitor on a regular basis. Again, these metrics are designed to lead to decisions to help the performance of this channel.

Key metrics that should be assessed with any reseller business model are as follows:

- **Percentage of revenue/deals sourced from channel partners (self-sufficient channel).** If you have made the investment in training for your partners to become truly self-sufficient, then what are the business contributions that come from these partners? A self-sufficient partner can manage the entire sales and marketing business process without any help from your company. This business relationship is a win-win for both parties, in that your company recognizes a lower cost of sales, and the partner recognizes greater commission fees. This measurement is very strategic, in that success here means you can grow revenue without investing in expensive internal sales resources.

- **Percentage of revenue outsourced to channel partners (non-self-sufficient partner community).** This measurement reflects your ability to outsource the process of closing business to your reseller community. This is basically a measurement of the bandwidth to close deal volume by leveraging external resources. As mentioned earlier, these channel partners are dependent on your company to feed them business, and since you still incur a healthy cost of sales in this model, the commission fee should be lower than for self-sufficient partners.

- **Partner/reseller cost of acquisition.** This metric determines the cost of customer acquisition for both reseller business models referenced above. The cost of acquisition for the partner community is similar to that for the internal sales and marketing organization. It can be calculated by simply dividing all the costs spent on acquiring more customers (internal channel sales and marketing expenses) by the number of customers acquired in the period the money was spent. You then can compare the cost of customer acquisition between internal and external business models. Over time, the cost of customer acquisition should go down as your partner community becomes more experienced with your company's value proposition.

- **Average margin for channel partners.** This metric is used to determine how profitable your reseller channel is to your company. It is a simple calculation of total revenue from channel partners divided by total expense in recruiting, managing, supporting, and retaining your reseller community. It is always an important exercise to compare the margin contribution from both internal and external sales channels. This measurement should improve over time as your partner community becomes more experienced with your company's value proposition.

- **Forecast accuracy by partner.** This is an interesting metric and is easy to measure. Compare the revenue and deal commitment from your channel partners independent of your internal channel sales team. Who is more accurate? Does one source tell you what you want to hear versus what is reality? If both sources are consistent in their revenue and deal projections and that consistency translates into accurate forecasts, then your channel sales organization is well aligned with your reseller community. If not, then appropriate actions are necessary to determine the root cause of the problem.

Again, many of the KPI metrics in this book can be applied to your channel partners. The key is clarity in regard to expectations and rules of engagement for your channel partners and operational consistency with forecast process disciplines for all internal and external sales resources.

CHAPTER 7

KEY PERFORMANCE INDICATORS FOR SALES EFFECTIVENESS AND EFFICIENCY

Embrace what you don't know, especially in the beginning, because what you don't know can become your greatest asset. It insures you will absolutely be doing things different from everybody else.
—Sara Blakely, SPANX founder

The more you understand the dynamics of your team's performance, the more you can make important decisions on the necessary sales investments to improve the effectiveness and efficiency of your personnel. I have used the following key performance indicators (KPIs) to assess the overall effectiveness and efficiency as well as the productivity of the sales organization:

- Sales and Marketing Effectiveness Ratio
- Productivity per Qualified Head Count
- Contribution Margin per Head Count
- Days Sales Outstanding (DSO)
- Sales Expense as a Percentage of Revenue
- Average Transaction Size by Rep/Product/Region
- Time Duration to Fully Qualify a Sales Representative

- Average Price per User
- Percentage of Sales Professionals Making Annual Quota
- Business Seasonality
- Competitive Analysis—Win/Loss Report
- Product Analysis—Percentage of Product Attainment by Quarter
- Cost of Sales Percentage
- Average Discount Rates per Quarter
- Pipeline Aging Ratio by Sales Stage
- Percentage of "No Decision" Losses

Let's explore why each of these key performance indicators is important by evaluating its merits individually.

- **Sales and Marketing Effectiveness Ratio**

Sales and Marketing Effectiveness Ratio = Total Revenue / Total Sales and Marketing Spent

Why is this KPI important? This is a simple measurement that needs to be assessed over time. It measures how effective your company is with the sales and marketing spent each quarter to achieve revenue results.

- **Productivity per Qualified Head Count**

Revenue / Qualified Head Count = Productivity per Head Count

Why is this KPI important? This is one of the most important key performance indicators in measuring the effectiveness and efficiency of the sales team. You should expect that as sales representatives gain more maturity in their sales discipline, their productivity over time should also improve. They should naturally get better at their jobs. But this also includes training and certification investments that impact productivity. When a company makes an investment in enhancing the expertise of their sales personnel, a measurement of the effectiveness of that training initiative should be reflected in their productivity. It should trend upward over multiple quarters, but it is not realistic to expect it to go up every quarter.

For example, if you look at the following graph, you see the productivity trending in a positive direction. I conducted a very significant training initiative in the third quarter (Q3) of 2017. As you can see, the productivity went down that quarter. This training required the entire sales team to be out of the territory for a solid week. I always mentioned how expensive these training events were to the company. It is not in the financial investment associated with the event but for the fact that the entire sales organization is not in the field selling our products to their customer base.

Productivity per Headcount:

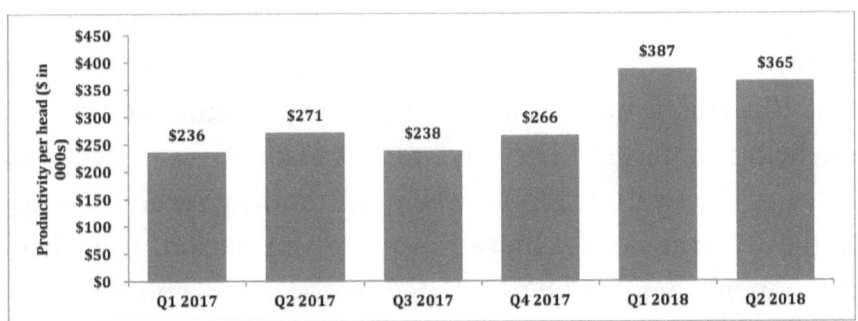

This calculation can be done in a number of ways. I typically use the calculation of total booked revenue divided by the qualified sales head count (sales personnel who have past onboarding training and have been with the company longer than ninety days) for the quarter. Qualified sales head count could also include presales and post-sales resources.

- **Contribution Margin per Head Count**

    Contribution Margin / Qualified Sales Head Count
    = Contribution Margin per Head Count

Why is this KPI important? The same analysis from the productivity-per-head count assessment can also be applied to contribution margin. Again, this is a solid measurement for the effectiveness and efficiency of the sales organization.

- **Days Sales Outstanding (DSO)**

DSO Ratio = Accounts Receivable / Average Sales per Day, or
DSO Ratio = Accounts Receivable / (Annual Sales / 365 Days)

Why is this KPI important? How successful the company is in collecting its outstanding account receivables can be measured in days sales outstanding. It is a calculation used by a company to estimate its average collection period. It is a financial ratio that illustrates how well a company's accounts receivables are being managed. The days sales outstanding figure is an index of the relationship between outstanding receivables and credit account sales achieved over a given period. It is also a component that can be negotiated by the sales representatives to ensure his or her company receives prompt payment. A sales representative can have a very significant impact on this measurement.

- **Sales Expense as a Percentage of Revenue**

Sales Expense / Total Revenue = Sales
Expense as Percentage of Revenue

Why is this KPI important? This is a valuable key performance indicator, but it is very difficult to measure and evaluate without outside benchmark analysis. How much to invest in sales as a percentage of revenue can change dramatically among companies even in the same industry. A key here is the maturity of the company. Early-stage start-ups will spend more on product development than sales and marketing for obvious reasons. As the product becomes more accepted in the marketplace, additional sales investments may be warranted.

Many other factors can influence this measurement, including a company's product user experience as well as the company's go-to-market business model. This is measured as salary, commission, and overhead of the sales team and many times may include marketing expenses.

- **Average Transaction Size by Rep/Product/Region**

Total Revenue / Number of Transactions
= Average Transaction Size

Why is this KPI important? Is the average transaction size growing for your organization? How about the average price per user? Is your discounting increasing every quarter? How about the number of deals over $50,000? Are these transactions growing each quarter? It is an important trend to track on a consistent basis. It could answer some very important questions regarding the effectiveness of your sales personnel. For example, if this key performance indicator is trending downward, it might be a sign that competitive pressures are causing your sales personnel to discount more in order to secure the business. How many deals have you lost in the quarter due to pricing? Is that captured in your sales force automation tool? It should be. Here is an example of tracking Average Transaction Size or Deals over $50,000:

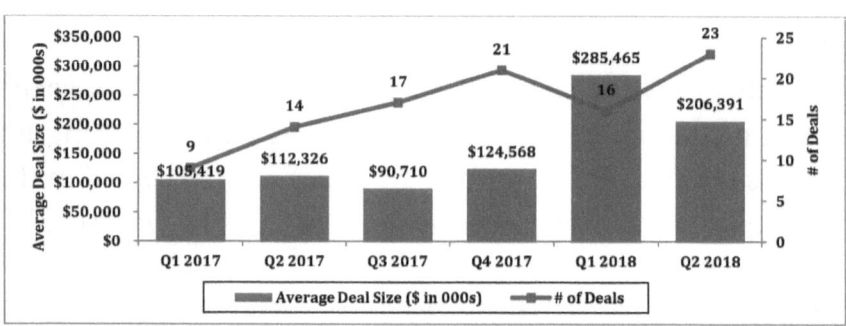

What made Q1 2018 so special? What can we learn from the success in this quarter versus the drop that occurred in Q3 2017? Was it a marketing campaign? Was it due to seasonality of the business? Did discounting play a role in these numbers? It is your responsibility to know these answers.

- **Time Duration to Fully Qualify a Sales Representative**

  Time in Months to Complete Training or
  Certification / Number of Qualified Head Count
  = Onboarding Time Frame for New Reps

Why is this KPI important? This key performance indicator is a measurement of the effectiveness of your sales representative onboarding process. This is the time it takes to certify the new sales hire into a fully productive member of the team. In the high-tech industry, this typically takes between ninety and 120 days for inside sales resources and as much as six months for field sales representatives. This will change based on the complexity of your company's products and services.

- **Average Price per User**

Total Revenue / Number of Users for Your
Product or Service = Average Price per User

Why is this KPI important? This measurement is critical to assessing the discount discipline of your sales team. If the average price per user is going down each quarter, it could imply that your sales team is discounting too much or that new competitive threats are forcing your team to change the pricing parameters of your products. If this is true, is your sales team adequately prepared to handle difficult objection questions that challenge the value of your solution from prospective customers without giving in to discount pressures?

- **Percentage of Sales Professionals Making Annual Quota**

Total Number of Reps Making Quota / Total Number of
All Sales Reps = Percentage of Quota-Attaining Reps

Why is this KPI important? This may be a measurement of the talent and expertise of your team to make their numbers. It also may be a measurement to assess the accuracy of your quota assignments. It is not realistic to believe that all sales personnel will make their annual quota objectives. If they do, it is a safe bet that your quota assignments were too low. Since you have many individuals who will both overachieve and underachieve their quotas, a target measurement that has worked for me in the past is for 70 percent of the sales personnel to make their annual targets. To me, this ensures the company will make its numbers and the quota was assigned accurately.

This measurement will be in direct correlation to the morale of the sales team. If this number continues to be low on a quarterly or annual basis, expect attrition to increase. It is far more economical to the company to keep good sales talent than to recruit and onboard new sales hires. Too many companies forget that fact.

- **Business Seasonality**

Although not a true key performance indicator, another consideration is the seasonality of your business. For example, in doing business with the federal government sector, you have to understand clearly the buying cycle associated with this market sector. Quarterly distribution of annual government revenue attainment typically is distributed differently than commercial accounts (For example: Q1 = 10 percent; Q2 = 15 percent; Q3 = 30 percent; Q4 = 45 percent).

Why is this KPI important? It is critical to understand the dynamics of seasonality and how it affects your business cycle. This could be a reflection of how your targeted industry buys your solution.

It is also not uncommon for customers to hold their purchases until the end of the quarter. I have experienced too many quarters where 80 percent of the business commitment was achieved over the last two weeks of the quarter. The customer understands the importance of sales personnel making their forecasts to their company and holds out until the end of the quarter as a negotiation ploy for deeper discounts. This dynamic is a reality in many businesses, and the more you understand and can manage this trend, the more accurate you will be with your sales forecasts.

- **Competitive Analysis—Win/Loss Report**

Number of Competitive Wins / Total sales
Engagements = Win Percentage

Why is this KPI important? This is a measurement that can provide great intelligence to your company on why you win and lose business. Who are your toughest competitors? Why do you lose to them? Are you losing business based on a lack of required functionality? Do you lose on price? Are your sales personnel being outsold? This should be tracked within your SFA/CRM system and monitored every week.

- **Product Analysis—Percentage of Product Attainment by Quarter**

Revenue by Product / Total Revenue =
Percentage of Product Attainment

Why is this KPI important? Out of the portfolio of solutions you offer to the market, what sells the best and why? What products have low sales and why? Is it the product capability or pricing? Is it because the sales personnel focus on better-selling products? Will a sales incentive fix this problem? Does the product require additional functionality?

This measurement is as important to the product development and engineering teams as it is to the sales organization.

- **Cost of Sales Percentage**

Total Sales Team Compensation Expense (Base Salary and Commission Incentives) / Revenues from Sales Attainment = Cost of Sales Percentage

Why is this KPI important? This is a simple calculation that can also be expanded to include other key revenue-producing expenses, such as marketing expense (demand generation), direct business expenses for sales, and corporate overhead. It is very different from how your finance department views the cost of sales measurement. Typically, the finance organization defines this measurement as the direct costs attributable to the production of the goods or supply of services by an entity. It is also commonly known as the cost of goods sold (COGS). Cost of sales measures the cost of goods produced or services provided in a period by an entity. This calculation will differ from business to business.

- **Average Discount Rates per Quarter**

List Price of All Products or Services Sold / Revenue Recognized = Average Discount Rate

Why is this KPI important? This is a measurement that should be tracked over time to assess the discount discipline of your team. It can also be reflected in the average price per user. If your price is going down and your discount rates are going up, you need to assess the root cause of the problem quickly. Your sales team could be ill prepared to defend their pricing versus more aggressive competitors.

- **Pipeline Aging Ratio by Sales Stage**

Duration of Deals / Revenue by Sales Stage = Pipeline Aging

Why is this KPI important? This is another measurement that should be tracked over time. Are your deals stuck in certain sales stages for weeks at a time? Is too much of your pipeline in early-sales-stage categories for too long? Do you have enough transactional pipeline in late-stage categories to make your quarterly commitment? Are your deals migrating at a productive pace through each sales stage, highlighting a healthy deal velocity?

When deals do not move in the pipeline, especially if they are in early stages, do not hesitate to eliminate them from your pipeline altogether. Don't get enamored by a large pipeline when in reality it is dramatically smaller since you did not have the discipline to eliminate stagnant business opportunities. Stagnant deals can be very misleading. Most successful deals have a rhythm and smooth migration from sales stage to sales stage. Long and extended sales cycles happen for a reason.

Time management is critical to any sales representative. Their time is truly reflective of their earning capability. Large deals still enamor many sales representatives with low probability of winning. Sales and marketing leaders must look for this and ensure their sales and marketing teams are working on high-probability opportunities. It is your responsibility to ensure your team prioritizes the right opportunities each quarter.

- **Percentage of "No Decision" Losses**

Total Deals Lost Due to No Decision / Total Deals Closed
in the Quarter = Percentage of "No Decision" Losses

Why is this KPI important? Make no mistake about the fact that a "no decision" is a loss and should be treated as such. These losses drain sales and marketing resources. It is also a poor reflection on your team's ability to qualify their business opportunities. It is imperative to constantly qualify the buying intentions of your prospective customers in each sales stage so that time is not wasted on deals that will never close.

CHAPTER 8

KEY PERFORMANCE INDICATORS FOR REVENUE FORECAST AND TREND ANALYSIS

In the end, a vision without the ability to execute it is probably a hallucination.

—Steve Case, AOL cofounder

As highlighted in the previous chapter, it is extremely important to track the performance trends of your sales personnel in order to improve the productivity of the team. It is equally important to track metrics to ensure forecast accuracy.

Make sure you understand the trending of your key performance indicators before you make expensive sales investment decisions. My sales operations team would always tell me that *the trend is my friend.* In the past, I decided to ignore the trend and convinced myself that I was going to make my numbers for the quarter. Every time, I was proven wrong. Ignore the trends of your business at your own risk.

There are seven key performance indicators that are critical for forecast accuracy. They are as follows:

- Percentage Attainment during the Quarter versus Weekly Targets
- Percentage of Committed Deals (dollar value) Deferred to Future Quarters
- Pipeline Coverage for Committed Quarterly Forecast by Sales Stage
- Close to Pipeline Ratio (quality pipeline or lack of rep coverage)
- Pipeline by Sales Stage versus Committed Forecast
- Percentage of the Forecast Change versus Commitment—Weekly Variance
- Average Sell Cycle by Product or Target Market

Understanding the dynamics of your sales engagement process, the productivity of your team, and the average transaction pricing will provide guidance on the most appropriate go-to-market strategy leveraging your sales resource investments.

- **Percentage Attainment during the Quarter versus Weekly Targets**

Revenue Attainment / Quarterly Quota =
Percentage of Attainment during the Quarter

Why is this KPI important? The trend is your friend because it never lies. We have talked about the importance of predictable revenue growth, but in many cases, that challenge for a company is not only in the revenue growth but also in accurate predictability. Today's economy makes it extremely difficult to be able to predict revenue attainment.

It is recommended that the pipeline and attainment for the quarter be assessed each and every week. Break each quarter into twelve-week increments (sometimes thirteen weeks based on the quarter). Track the performance of the team over multiple quarters and assess the trend analysis of your team. For example, my experience has shown that the pipeline coverage should be as follows for key strategic weeks:

- week 2 (first critical forecast of record for the quarter): 3X to 4X pipeline coverage to committed forecast
- week 6 (critical week to communicate to analysts if the company is public): 2.25X pipeline coverage to committed forecast
- week 10 (must be accurate to 1–3 percent to the final attainment of the quarter): 1.25X pipeline coverage to committed forecast

The same can apply to attainment. In the high-tech industry, it is not uncommon to have only 20 percent of your committed bookings closed by week 10 of the quarter. The backend nature of business attainment should be anticipated, and panic should not set in with the management team when this trend is clearly understood.

Consider that each quarter you can track trends will greatly assist your predictability. Each week, two things are sure to occur:

Your pipeline should decrease over the course of the quarter since your team should be closing business. You may see some spikes due to large deals that enter the current quarter pipeline during the quarter, but your sales team is responsible for keeping accurate pipeline records and for closing deals in the backlog.

What should be your pipeline coverage after the first month of the quarter? How about the second month? How much pipeline should be available during the critical last month of the quarter? How does this compare with your most successful quarters? How about your most disappointing quarters?

Attainment for the quarter is increasing. This is an obvious point, but critical in the predictability of your quarter is that you track this measurement every quarter. For example, what percentage of your quarterly commitment has closed in week 4? How about week 8 or week 10? Why is this important?

Based on these two events, what can you conclude about the success or failure of your quarter? If you have been tracking these events each week for the past few quarters, you can establish important trends in the efforts to establish predictability in your business.

Ask yourself some key questions about the trends of your quarterly attainment. What is the targeted pipeline you wish to have at the beginning of every quarter? What about your attainment percentage during the same time frame? Does the pipeline reflect a healthy coverage to your committed outlook? How about in week 4? Your first month of the quarter is over. How does it compare with week 4 in your best quarter? How about in week 8? Your second quarter is just completed. How does it compare with your best quarter? How much business typically closes during the last few weeks of the quarter?

The following graph represents this important trend. Notice the analysis of the pipeline decreasing and the attainment trend as it compares to previous quarters. This weekly analysis and clear understanding of the trends of your business attainment can be the difference in making your business commitments or losing credibility within your company for missing an important revenue forecast.

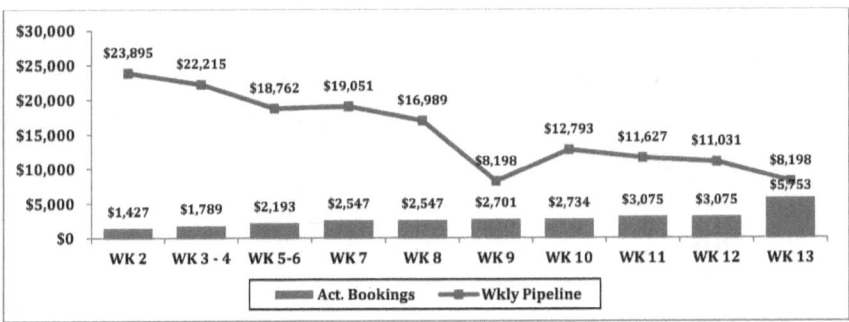

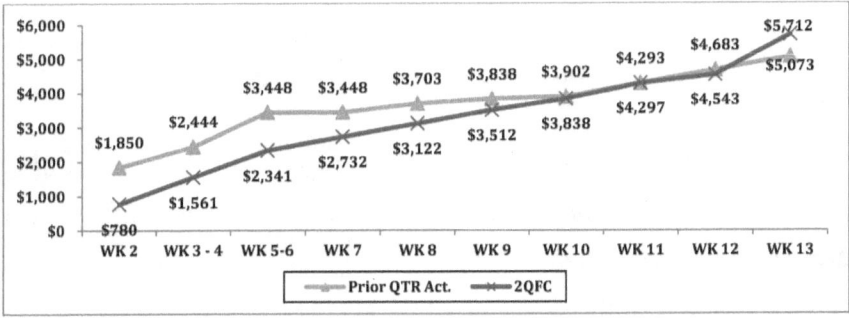

- **Percentage of Committed Deals (Dollar Value) Deferred to Future Quarters**

Revenue Associated with Deferred Deals / Total Revenue for the Quarter = Percentage of Deferred Committed Deals

Why is this KPI important? It is important to determine how many transactions defer from the committed forecast to the following quarter. It is important to send a message to your team that this practice is unacceptable. Most often, deals are deferred due to a lack of execution of the sales individual in managing the sales engagement process. Most often, I would challenge the sales representative that the deal must be closed within the first thirty days of the following quarter. Track this key performance indicator very closely since it is a reflection of the professionalism of your team. Another measurement you can add here is the close percentage of deferred deals during first month of next quarter: Total deals deferred that were closed in first month ($) / percentage of deals deferred from previous quarter = close percentage of deferred deals.

- **Pipeline Coverage for Committed Quarterly Forecast by Sales Stage**

Total Pipeline ($) / Committed Forecast to the Business = Pipeline Coverage

Why is this KPI important? The first step in sales accountability is to understand the dynamics of your pipeline early in the quarter. Start by assessing your overall backlog of opportunities that have been flagged as potential deals in the quarter. You will also need to determine what percent coverage is acceptable for your business. I have always used the 3X minimum test. This means, do I have the overall dollar value of my pipeline that exceeds my quarterly revenue objective by 3X or greater? To me, a healthy backlog to start a quarter was always between 3X and 4X, assuming the pipeline data was accurate. That gave me assurance that I had enough deals in the works to cover my sales commitment for the quarter. Your business may dictate a larger or smaller pipeline coverage ratio.

Please note that a 3X pipeline coverage model is an estimate and not to be used for all scenarios. The required pipeline coverage for a sales representative or a region is in direct correlation to their close rate. A high close rate dictates a lower pipeline coverage model. It also represents a higher quality pipeline with key opportunities reflected in later sales stages.

This obviously also assumes that your close rate is 33 percent as a trend to monitor over time. For example, if your quota was $10M for the quarter and your traditional close rate was about 33 percent, you should have at least $30M or 3X coverage at the beginning of the quarter to ensure your success in achieving this milestone. Management should track the performance of each member of his or her team to determine the historical close rate of the organization. I found that typically my team had a close rate of about 32–36 percent each quarter, so a 3X coverage model was satisfactory to make my quarterly objectives.

Pipeline coverage to committed forecast or quota objectives along with a clear understanding of the track record of your team in regard to close rates are the first steps in assessing the success of your quarter. The chart below is a typical pipeline assessment on the first day of the quarter. It represents the total pipeline on the first day of the quarter, broken down by sales stage. What conclusions can be drawn based on this simple chart?

The total revenue pipeline for the current quarter is as follows:

$ in USD	Sales Regio ▾				
Sales Stage ▾	US Central & Canada	US East	US Government	US West	Grand Total
01 - Identify Prospect - 0%	$ 1,019,446	$ 140,000	$ 102,070	$ 285,000	$ 1,546,516
02 - Initial Contact - 5%	$ 326,102	$ 12,387	$ 120,938	$ 252,000	$ 711,427
03 - Qualify Customer Interest - 30%	$ 2,167,119	$ 3,167,948	$ 2,587,864	$ 1,474,279	$ 9,397,210
04 - Identify Requirements - 40%	$ 1,650,152	$ 2,042,834	$ 1,680,954	$ 1,684,972	$ 7,058,912
05 - Determine Solution - 50%	$ 2,402,801	$ 1,643,431	$ 1,748,007	$ 1,345,397	$ 7,139,635
06 - Present Proposal - 60%	$ 1,501,107	$ 3,401,708	$ 3,506,378	$ 1,652,605	$10,061,799
07 - Negotiate to Close - 70%	$ 791,061	$ 1,199,711	$ 3,074,731	$ 429,645	$ 5,495,149
Grand Total	$ 9,857,788	$ 11,608,018	$ 12,820,943	$ 7,123,898	$41,410,647

First of all, the total pipeline is approximately $41M in overall dollar value. Assuming that my team has a close rate that fluctuates between 32 percent and 36 percent each quarter, I can assume my overall attainment should be approximately about $13.5M to $14.7M for the quarter. There is nothing magical to this analysis. If your pipeline data is clean and accurate in regard to your opportunities within the quarter, this simple calculation (total pipeline x close rate) should reflect the potential for success during the quarter.

Your team's close rate will fluctuate by region. Some members of your team may be more conservative than others, so it is recommended to track traditional close rates by each sales entity. This could be individual sales representatives or a manager. In the example in this chapter, we highlighted a regional sales organization. You typically do not want to see fluctuations in the region's close rate by more than 10 percent each quarter. Wide fluctuation in quarterly close rates is a sign that the region has a sales execution problem and is probably unreliable with their forecast accuracy.

From this analysis, it also appears that the breakdown of this attainment by region should be as follows:

East Region: This region has been very accurate in its forecast projections over the last few quarters and has averaged 33.6 percent close rate each quarter over that time. With a total pipeline of approximately $11.6M, it appears that the initial forecast of the quarter should be about $3.89M.

Central Region: This region has not been very accurate in its forecast projections over the last few quarters and has averaged only 27.5 percent close rate each quarter over that time. With close rates fluctuating significantly each quarter, you have less confidence in this region's ability to make its initial outlook. This may be a sign that your sales management in this region does not have the required visibility into their business as do your other regions. With a total pipeline of approximately $9.8M, it appears that the initial forecast of the quarter should be about $2.69M. This outlook has risk since the close rate fluctuates by greater than 20 percent each quarter.

West Region: This region has also been accurate in its forecast projections over the last few quarters and has averaged 38.3 percent close rate each quarter over that time. With a total pipeline of approximately $7.1M, it appears that the initial forecast of the quarter should be about $2.71M. This brings up another important observation. The west region has a close rate that is exceptionally high in comparison to the other regions. This may be a sign of a very strong sales team that has the skills and expertise to close the deals targeted for the quarter. It may also mean that the total pipeline is at a too conservative number compared to the other regions. The importance of consistency with the data across all regions can't be understated. It may also represent that the lead generation contribution to the quarter is at an unacceptable level.

Government Region: This region has fluctuated each quarter in attainment very dramatically but for a different reason. Typically the federal government sector experiences significant seasonality of their business. We addressed this issue in more detail earlier in the book, but traditionally it is anticipated that your annual attainment from the government business reflects the federal government buying cycle, which is heavily weighted toward year-end acquisitions. Many of the federal government's decisions in regard to IT expenditures typically happen during the months of September and October.

The government region is expected to close at an average rate of 36.2 percent, so with a total pipeline of approximately $12.8M, it appears that the initial forecast of the quarter should be about $4.63M.

These are very simple measurements, but the first step is assessing your sales predictability for the quarter.

- **Close to Pipeline Ratio (Quality Pipeline or Lack of Rep Coverage)**

  Total Pipeline x Trending Close Rate = Close Percentage

Why is this KPI important? The previous example highlights the importance of tracking the specific close rate of your team. Understanding the historical average will be critical to assessing your team's forecasting accuracy and the amount of visibility your sales executives has into their business.

For example, look at the chart highlighted below to see what the close rate has been for the east region over time. Based on past performance, the cumulative average for this region is approximately 37 percent.

East Region Close Rate Analysis:

	Q1	Q2	Q3	Q4
Pipeline @ Week 1 of Quarter:	$ 10,500,000	$12,300,000	$14,800,000	$17,200,000
Actual Attainment during the Quarter:	$ 3,590,000	$ 4,789,990	$ 5,763,450	$ 6,135,900
Close Rate:	34%	39%	39%	36%
Cumulative Average:	37%			

It is also important to realize that this metric tells you a great deal about the process discipline surrounding the management of the pipeline within a specific region. For example, if the close rate falls dramatically below the cumulative average for your team, it may represent that the pipeline has inaccurate data, which is misrepresenting the true opportunity for the quarter. The sales executives for that specific region may not be putting in the time to keep the status of their potential deals in the pipeline current. If the pipeline is inaccurate, then the close rate is inaccurate.

This is all about commitment to the sales process disciplines within that specific region and potentially a lack of leadership by the sales management responsible for this region. If 80 percent of the regional team have the discipline to keep their pipeline data accurate and 20 percent are negligent with these responsibilities, then you will at best be only 80 percent accurate with your forecast accuracy. This is why the best sales organizations make this responsibility a requirement for employment. You may have an individual who has great selling skills but could hurt the credibility of the organization without the process discipline associated with managing his or her pipeline data.

A poor close rate may also reflect that the skills and expertise of the sales personnel in that region are not sufficient to succeed on a consistent basis. This might be a warning sign that you need an investment in sales training or a heightened focus on performance management.

It may also reflect that you do not have the head count to cover the opportunity within the region. Assuming that the pipeline data accurately reflects the potential deals for the quarter, you may have a sales coverage problem in that you do not have the required sales resources to successfully close the deals for the quarter. This is certainly a good problem to have since adding head count is a sign of a healthy and prosperous business.

To assess this concern, you must evaluate the sales cycle duration of your products and services in light of the opportunity represented in the pipeline. For example, if the sell cycle (time it takes from the point where an opportunity is identified to the time when contracts are signed and revenue is recognized) is six to nine months and a specific individual has twenty-five prospects, all with good-size deals in various stages of the sell cycle, can this sales executive really accurately cover all the opportunity reflected in his or her pipeline? Maybe the sell cycle is artificially too long since this person can't professionally manage more than a half-dozen deals at one time. Would additional head count reduce the sell cycle duration and enhance coverage of the territory? Would the territory be less prone to competitive threats?

These are all valid questions to ask when assessing the quality of the pipeline and the ability to deliver the required revenue for the quarter.

- **Pipeline by Sales Stage versus Committed Forecast**

$$\text{Sales Stage Commitment} / \text{Total Pipeline}$$
$$= \text{Sales Stage Commitment}$$

Why is this KPI important? Another step in assessing the quality of your pipeline is to determine how much of your business is in what sales stage. Obviously, if the majority of your business is in the early stages of a sell cycle (stages 1 through 3) and typically your products have a sell cycle time frame of three to six months, then you will have a very challenging time exceeding your quarterly objective. On the other hand, if the majority of your business potential for the quarter is in the final three sales stages (stages 5 through 7), you will probably be well positioned for a successful quarter.

Your first step is to determine the sales stage definitions. Many sales force automation tools provide these measurements. For this example, the sales stages fall under these categories (highlighted in chapter 3):

- **Identify prospect**. Initial stage opportunity that has been qualified by your team. Qualification may take the form of validating that the customer has plans for an acquisition, has the appropriate budget, and will consider your company's solution.

- **Qualify initial vision alignment.** Your company has been selected to bid on the proposed solution.
- **Identify business needs/requirements.** Your sales team has a strong understanding of the requirements of the solution, and your company will be competitive in the evaluation.
- **Confirm the buying process.** Your sales team clearly understands the procurement process of the customer.
- **Determine solution.** Your proposal is tailored for the customer, and the solution is very competitive.
- **Present proposal.** The proposal is presented to customer executives, and all objections have been addressed.
- **Negotiate to close.** The customer has made a decision to acquire your solution, and the final step is to finalize legal negotiations.

Once you have defined the sales stage, you need to determine the odds of closing the deal based on the appropriate percentages for each stage. Keep in mind you may be in the late stages of a sales engagement but have a low percentage of closing the transaction. Never associate a sales stage with a probability percentage of closing the deal. They are independent assessments of the transaction.

An example is as follows:

10 percent. The opportunity has been identified and qualified in that the customer has a planned acquisition time frame and has budget identified.

20 percent. Your company has been selected to bid on the business. An RFP (request for proposal) or RFQ (request for quotation) may have been released.

30 percent. The initial value proposition from your solution has been well received by either the key decision makers or the individuals who will influence the decision.

40 percent. The competitive advantages of your proposal are clearly understood by the customer. The customer has set up a timeline for a decision.

50 percent. A proof of concept (POC) or trial, if required, has been completed with positive results.

60 percent. The customer has called or conducted a site visit to one of your referenced clients and came away impressed with your solution.

70 percent. Proposal has been evaluated, and the customer executives are impressed with your proposal, including proposed pricing.

80 percent. Customer has selected your solution.

90 percent. Contract negotiations have begun, and no issues are anticipated.

100 percent. Contracts are signed, and your company has recognized revenue.

So let's take a look at the sales organizations highlighted below and make some observations on the health of their pipeline.

The total revenue pipeline for the current quarter is as follows:

$ in USD	Sales Region				
Sales Stage	US Central & Canada	US East	US Government	US West	Grand Total
01 - Identify Prospect - 0%	$ 1,019,446	$ 140,000	$ 102,070	$ 285,000	$ 1,546,516
02 - Initial Contact - 5%	$ 326,102	$ 12,387	$ 120,938	$ 252,000	$ 711,427
03 - Qualify Customer Interest - 30%	$ 2,167,119	$ 3,167,948	$ 2,587,864	$ 1,474,279	$ 9,397,210
04 - Identify Requirements - 40%	$ 1,650,152	$ 2,042,834	$ 1,680,954	$ 1,684,972	$ 7,058,912
05 - Determine Solution - 50%	$ 2,402,801	$ 1,643,431	$ 1,748,007	$ 1,345,397	$ 7,139,635
06 - Present Proposal - 60%	$ 1,501,107	$ 3,401,708	$ 3,506,378	$ 1,652,605	$10,061,799
07 - Negotiate to Close - 70%	$ 791,061	$ 1,199,711	$ 3,074,731	$ 429,645	$ 5,495,149
Grand Total	$ 9,857,788	$ 11,608,018	$ 12,820,943	$ 7,123,898	$41,410,647

It is easy to determine what region has the healthiest pipeline. The government region not only has the largest total pipeline ($12.8M in business opportunities), but approximately 50 percent of the opportunities are in sales stage 6 and 7. The only concern would be if only a few large opportunities were represented in these stages. For example, if one transaction representing $2M+ is represented in sales stage 6 and the deal does not occur, then your analysis that was once optimistic is now very concerning.

- **Percentage of the Forecast Change versus Commitment— Weekly Variance**

Forecasted Business Commitment versus
Revised Forecast Commitment

Why is this KPI important? Another reflection of the professionalism of your sales team is their ability to accurately forecast and honor their business commitments. If you see wide variations in their weekly forecasts, that is a sign that the sales representative or manager does not understand the dynamics of his or her pipeline. It could also be indicative of a lack of focus regarding the process disciplines associated with the sales engagement process. It is easy to forecast a low number in week 2 and a larger, more accurate number in week 10 when the attainment for the quarter is clearer. Unfortunately, C-level management will not allow this behavior. The CFOs of public companies have to provide revenue guidance in week 6 and are looking to the sales leadership to help with this assessment. I always liked this discipline and used it even with small start-ups and nonpublic companies.

Track the fluctuations of the weekly forecast. Hold each sales individual accountable. I held my teams accountable to be within 10 percent of the final attainment in the week 6 forecast and no more that 1–3 percent from the week 10 forecast commitment. Tracking this weekly heightens visibility into the business and holds your team accountable to honor their business commitments.

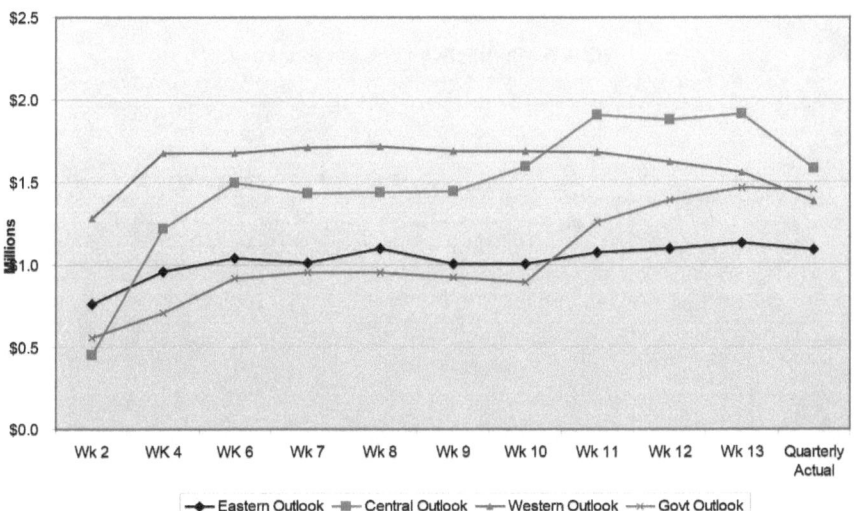

North America Regional Accuracy

You will see that the regional forecasts increase over the quarter. This is a safe way of forecasting since it assumes no risk. As mentioned earlier, your CFO will not stand for this method of forecasting from you as the sales leader. Why would you allow your team to forecast in this unproductive manner?

Here is an example of this bad forecast behavior when you look at the rolled-up forecast in the next graph. It is clear that the VP of North American sales is assuming all the risk in the early weeks of the quarter. The committed forecast from the VP is approximately $5.5M where the regional forecast only adds up to an unacceptable $3M. The VP used past trend analysis to understand how his regions typically forecasted their business. This is a great opportunity to coach and mentor your team on the expectation of the forecast process and the importance of accurately forecasting business commitments early in the quarter. It shows that you know your business and are a professional sales executive.

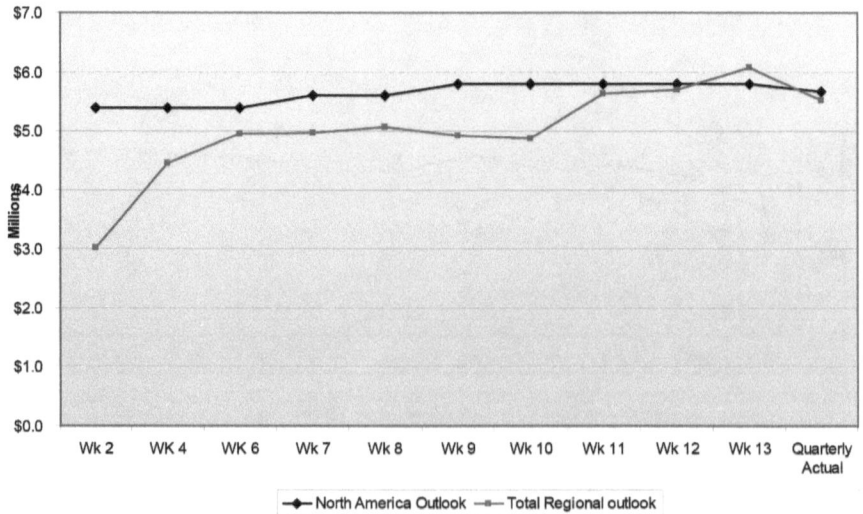

2Q04 North America Forecast Accuracy

- **Average Sell Cycle by Product or Target Market**

Time from Opportunity Identification to Transaction Closure

Why is this KPI important? This measurement will fluctuate by sales resources and by target markets. The sell cycle (time it takes from the point where an opportunity is identified to the time when contracts are signed and revenue is recognized) will be longer for large-enterprise deals that require multiple levels of approval than for smaller midmarket or small, medium business transactions.

It is important that any sales leader understand the duration it takes to close transactions in order to assess sales efficiency within his or her team as well as the dynamics associated with targeted market segments.

CHAPTER 9

SALES TOOLS

To succeed in business, to reach the top, an individual must know all it is possible to know about that business.
— J. Paul Getty, Business Icon

This chapter is dedicated to providing valuable sales tools that will assist in the improvement of the sales predictability and accountability of your sales organization. The tools include the following:

1. **Sales Empowerment Grid.** A tool that will provide clarity to your sales personnel on what they can and can't do within a sales engagement process.
2. **Territory/Opportunity Plan.** This document represents the required components of an effective territory plan.
3. **Qualification Sales Questions.** Questions to probe/ learn more about the executive(s) in your meeting and to qualify your business opportunity.
4. **Opportunity Qualifying Checklist.** This template provides guidance on when a transaction should be moved into the quarterly forecast.

5. **Opportunity Plan Components.** Documented action plan to close a specific opportunity.

Each of the following documents can be tailored to represent your specific job descriptions and business requirements. Remember that one size does not fit all scenarios. The concept and motivation behind these documents apply to all companies regardless of the size. Take these documents and tailor them to serve your business requirements. The objective here is to improve the effectiveness and efficiency of the sales management process. It should also assist in improving the productivity of your sales resources.

Here are examples of the five tools referenced throughout this book:

1. Sales Empowerment Grid

Job Descriptions:

RAM:	Regional Account Manager
AE:	Account Executive (Inside Sales)
CSM:	Channel Sales Manager
CM:	Country Manager
MD:	Managing Director
VP:	Vice President

Discounting Procedures:

The following discount structure shall apply to the following job descriptions at XYZ:

Authority	Discount Off List
RAM, AE	5%
MD	10%
VP	15%
SVP	20%
CEO	20%+

Sales Operations will coordinate escalation of discount in excess of 20%.

Each request will require a documented close plan.

Sales Force Automation/Customer Relationship Management (SFA/CRM) Tool Commitment:

1. The proper use of the SFA/CRM tools is a condition of employment for all sales personnel.
2. Every member of the sales organization is expected to use this tool daily to record sales engagement records.
3. All sales personnel must adhere to usage guidelines, as documented by sales operations, of this tool to ensure consistency across all sales resources.
4. No commissions will be paid on any transaction that is not clearly documented within the SFA/CRM system.

Credit Terms:

1. SVP of sales must approve any credit term exception beyond thirty days.
2. CFO must approve any credit term exception beyond sixty days.

Contract Signatures—Contracts, Reseller Agreements, Nondisclosure Agreements:

1. Regional sales management can sign standard agreements without modifications.
2. Any nonstandard request must be approved by finance and legal. Signature authority will be sales SVP or CFO.
3. SVP of sales must sign nondisclosure agreements.

Market Development Funding (MDF):

1. Sales SVP and CFO must approve all MDF funding.
2. Once approved, regional sales management can make disbursement decisions without any further approval process.
3. Field marketing personnel will track invoices and authorization.

Revenue Recognition:

1. No side letters for any transaction will be allowed and could lead to termination.
2. The finance department must accept the order before commissions are paid.
3. Evidence of a financial transaction must exist.
4. The fee must be fixed or determinable.
5. Delivery of all transaction elements must occur.
6. Collection of the receivable must be probable.

Don Beck

Approval Authority Matrix:

Signature(s) Required [1]	Operating Expense [4]	
	Budgeted [7]	Unbudgeted [8]
CEO	>$100,000	>$20,000
President	>$50,000	>$15,000
Group Executive [2]	>$25,000	>$10,000
VP & GM [3]	>$10,000	>$5,000
Director	>$5,000	>$2,000
Manager	>$2,500	>$500

Signature(s) Required [1]	Capital Purchases [5]	
	Budgeted [7]	Unbudgeted [8]
CEO	>$100,000	>$20,000
President	>$50,000	>$15,000
Group Executive [2]	>$25,000	>$10,000
VP & GM [3]	>$5,000	>$2,500
Director	>$0	>$0
Manager	-	-

Signature(s) Required [1]	Contracts & Agreements [10]	
	Value	Duration
CEO	>$100,000	>2 yr & >$50k
President	>$50,000	>1 yr & >$25k
Group Executive [2]	>$25,000	>1 yr & >$15k
VP & GM [3]	>$5,000	>1 yr & >$2.5k
Director	>$0	-
Manager	-	-

Other Items	Signature(s) Required
> $5,000 Expense Report [11]	Functional Group VP and VP Finance
> Sixty-Day-Late Expense Report	Functional Group VP and VP Finance
Purchase of any financial derivative instrument	VP of Finance or CAO
<$25,000 Outgoing Wire	VP of Finance
>$25,000 Outgoing Wire	COO or CAO
Hiring Employee Budgeted	Functional Group VP and CAO
Hiring Employee Unbudgeted	CEO and CAO

[1] Signature approval may be in the form of e-mail or a signature on any company form, or vendor receipt or PO. All required titles are corporate-level titles and not subsidiary.

[2] Group executive includes the most senior executive for following functional groups: sales, marketing, R&D, business development, and administration.

[3] Regional sales VPs and country managers are considered directors for this authority matrix.

[4] Operating expenses include all items that will be immediately expensed in the income statement. All invoices in any thirty-day period from one vendor or for a specific project will be considered against the thresholds. Please contact the Finance Department if you need clarification for an operating expense versus a capital purchase.

[5] Capital purchases include all purchases that will be capitalized over a useful life. All invoices in any thirty-day period from one vendor or for a specific project will be considered against the thresholds. The functional VP of IT will have group executive approval for IT equipment capital purchases.

[6] SCM purchases are all purchases of materials related to the production of products.

[7] Required signature must be from the budgeting group's manager, director, VP, or group executive pursuant to the level required.

[8] Unbudgeted items below C-level approval require additional approval of VP Finance.

[9] Forecasted for SCM equals SCM purchases required to meet most current three-month sales forecast, and unforecasted equals any SCM purchase above the most current three-month sales forecast.

[10] Includes all leases and service obligations. All contracts and agreements > $10,000 or with duration > one year or both require legal review before execution.

[11] All expense reports in any thirty-day period will be considered against $5,000 threshold.

2. Territory/Opportunity Planning

XYZ Strategic Account Plan

I. Customer Name: Spartan Pharmaceuticals

- List Spartan Pharmaceuticals' corporate objectives.
- List Spartan Pharmaceuticals' corporate strategies and initiatives to achieve those objectives.
- List Spartan Pharmaceuticals' challenges and inhibitors to achieve those objectives.
- List Spartan Pharmaceuticals' needs and investment requirements to successfully achieve those objectives.
- What is XYZ's strategy to contribute to the success of Spartan Pharmaceuticals' corporate objectives?

II. Customer Business Profile

- What is the perception of XYZ Company at Spartan Pharmaceuticals?
- What current products and services are used by Spartan Pharmaceuticals?
- What business relationships do we have with Spartan Pharmaceuticals?
  - Client name and title?
  - Relationship status?

○ Scope of responsibility: Executive sponsor? Decision maker? Influencer? Inhibitor?
○ What relationship do they have with XYZ's competition?

III. XYZ Account Strategy

- goals: measurable/aggressive yet achievable
- strategies: key approaches to achieve goals
- initiatives: specific, funded projects to achieve defined goals
- opportunity qualification (see qualification checklist)
  ○ Why do something?
  ○ Why now?
  ○ Why with XYZ Company?
- partner/channel strategy
  ○ What channel partners have existing relationships with Spartan Pharmaceuticals that we can leverage?
- competitive intelligence
  ○ What strategy is in place to win against the competition?

IV. Account Opportunity Assessment

- Current business opportunities for XYZ at Spartan Pharmaceuticals?
  ○ Business/functional unit?
  ○ Executive sponsor?
  ○ Business opportunity for XYZ?
  ○ Close date?
  ○ Competition?
  ○ Value ($)?

- Twelve-Month Expansion Opportunities?
  - Business/functional unit?
  - Potential executive sponsor/relationship?
  - Potential solution?
  - Qualifying actions?
  - Resources needed?
  - Potential value?
  - Sales/marketing investments required?

V. Action Items

- Task?
- Who within XYZ is assigned responsibility?
- Committed time to completion?
- Status?

3. Qualification Sales Questions

Questions to probe/learn more about the executive(s) in your meeting and to qualify your business opportunity:

- **Can you describe the scope of your responsibility as (customer title)?**
  Most executives feel comfortable in talking about themselves and their responsibilities. It is a great way to open dialogue with a customer where we do not have a relationship. Attempt to determine the level of accountability this executive has in a decision for your company. Let him or her talk. Listen carefully.

- **How long have you been in your current position? During this time, how have your priorities changed?**
  Attempt to determine how his or her role has evolved at his or her employer.

- **What is your most pressing challenge in your current responsibilities? What keeps you up at night?**
  Every senior executive has pain points. Don't make the assumption that your solution is the most pressing initiative on this person's mind.

- **How does this project rank in importance to the challenges you just mentioned?**
  Determine the importance associated with your company's proposed solution to other priorities of the prospective client.

- **How will your success be measured in your current role?**
  If you can contribute to an executive's success, you will have a friend for life. Find out how you can make this executive look good through your services.

- **Can you describe the reporting structure of your current organization? What level of involvement will the person you report to have in regard to the evaluation or decision? Who involved in the project has the highest rank and greatest influence?**
  Determine the reporting structure to assess who is a gatekeeper, influencer, decision maker, or signature authority.

- **Who are the key people in your organization I could talk to who would provide me with a more detailed understanding of the problem or the current state?**
  With this question, you are volunteering to talk to lower levels of the organization to assess the details of the problem and current state. You are also positioning yourself as a key resource for the executive to leverage within the sales engagement. It is the first step toward achieving trusted adviser status with the targeted executive.

Questions to determine the requirements of the purchase:

- **Who is driving the business requirements of the proposed solution? Who initiated the project?**
  Determine what line of business is funding the initiative. Do you have access to these executives? Is there a centralized group that manages compliance and risk?

- **What is the most important problem you are trying to solve? Who will be most affected by the outcome of the project?**
  Don't get hung up on a feature or technology function. What is their real reason for investing in your company? Who in the customer organization will gain the most from the success of the project?

- **How will success be measured with the completion of this project?**
  Determine what proof points are required to justify the capability of your solution. Is it financially driven or tied back to a business milestone?

- **When is it desired to have the project in production? What is the compelling event behind this milestone?**
  A compelling event will determine a sense of urgency.

- **How does funding get secured for a project of this magnitude? Who is ultimately paying for this solution?**

- **How would you prioritize the requirements of the solution you desire?**
  Determine how well your solution addresses the requirements of the desired solution. Learn about the current methods of managing their infrastructure today. What does it look like?

- **How do you address these requirements today? Have you benchmarked your current status?**
  Determine if we will be able to qualify and quantify the specific benefits of your alternative.

- **What effect has the lack of a solution had on your organization?**
  Use the knowledge gained from this research to provide TCO (total cost of ownership) or ROI (return on investment) justification.

- **What have you done to address this problem?**
  Why are they evaluating your solution? Has the current process been benchmarked from effectiveness or cost/benefit perspective?

Questions to determine the timing of the decision and who is capable of making it:

- **Who will be involved with the evaluation of each alternative under consideration?**
  Determine what the circle of influence on this decision is and who you will need to establish relationships with in this engagement.

- **How many alternatives will be evaluated?**
  Determine who your competition is with this engagement.

- **How will the decision be made, and could you describe each step of the process?**
  Determine each step on how selection, funding, and legal negotiations will be done with this engagement. Learn how the decision process works and their current timeline. Is the current project budgeted, or is it still in planning stages?

- **Who will be involved with the process?**
  Who is the most important person associated with each step of the decision and procurement process?

- **How long does it take for a transaction of this size to typically go through your legal process? Procurement process?**
  Try to assess the time associated with these critical tasks of the customer's buying cycle.

- **Who will ultimately have the signature authority for this initiative?**
  Can you get access to the person who will have the signature authority for the transaction?

Questions to determine their level of interest in your company:

- **How much do you know about our company? How did your hear about us?**
  Determine if they heard about you from a current client or if they are truly interested in a managed service alternative.

4. Opportunity Qualifying Checklist

Sales Representative: Date: Est. Bookings $:
Customer: Close Month: Solution:

Can I forecast this deal?	Yes	No	N/A	Comments
Have we clearly qualified the opportunity?				
Is there a compelling event or business drivers?				
Have they clearly identified their requirements? Documented?				
Is top management aware and in agreement with these requirements?				
Has funding been identified/ secured? Budgeted for current quarter?				
Have decision criteria been established? Documented?				
Is the decision maker/signature authority available to us?				
Are we getting the necessary time with all key executives?				

All levels agree they need to act?

Is there risk in *not* acting? What are the consequences of doing nothing?

Doe we understand all aspects of the customer's decision criteria?

Have our credentials been established with all?

Do they have an active trial? When will it conclude?

Does our solution address their business requirements?

Can you articulate our client-specific business value propositions?

Does our solution fit their architectural/IT standards?

Have they expressed interest in or approval of our solution?

Is the decision maker biased to us? To a competitor?

Does any competitor have an advantage?

Are we competitive? Have they said so?

Was the trial a success—in *their* opinion?

Have preferences for our solution/us been stated?

If a partner is involved, do they have influence?

Other outside influences bear on their selection? Consultant?

Can we win this deal and predict its close date?

Are the business drivers *pressing*?

Do the decision makers have a sense of urgency?

Have the steps in the decision process (close plan) been agreed upon? In writing? With dates?			
Is there a *documented* project schedule?			
Are any interim steps required?			
Has a decision date been set?			
Is justification present, understood, and agreed upon?			
Has a date for realization of results been set?			
Is there risk in delay?			

5. Opportunity Plan Components

- **Clear understanding of the customer pain.** How can our products or services alleviate this problem for our prospective customer? Can we clearly articulate the customer requirements for this purchase?

- **GAP analysis on customer requirements to solution capability.** What are the odds of us winning this opportunity?

- **Is the opportunity qualified?**
  - Will the customer act?
  - Will the customer act *now*?
  - Will the customer act with us?

- **Define the competitive landscape.** Who will we compete with, and how do we compare from a competitive differentiation?

- **Identify resource requirements.** What resources will be needed both internally and externally to win this business?

- **Relationship assessment.** Do we have any relationships with the influencers and decision makers for this purchase?

- **Understanding the customer buying process.** Do we clearly understand the customer buying process and the criteria the potential customer will use to evaluate our solution's value proposition?

- **Documented action plan.** Have we identified each step required to win this business? Has this plan been presented and approved by management?

CHAPTER 10

CONCLUSION

Turn a perceived risk into an asset.
—Aaron Patzer, Mint founder

So how often should you assess the key measurements to running your business? That is only for you to decide, but it is important to remember the following words of Lou Gerstner, former CEO of IBM, which he wrote in his book, *Who Says Elephants Can't Dance?*

> At McKinsey my colleagues and I were constantly frustrated to see one company after another invest thousands of hours and millions of dollars to develop solid, effective statements of strategic direction and then waste all the time and money because the CEO was unwilling to drive change through the organization. At other times, the CEO thought change was taking place in the organization but failed to inspect what, in fact, was going on.

Perhaps the greatest mistake I've seen executives make is to confuse expectations with inspection.

He concludes that *people respect what you inspect.*

To avoid analysis paralysis, I would recommend the selection of your most important key performance indicators. To begin, take these following steps to establish a clearly understood process that your sales and marketing teams must embrace to achieve sales predictability.

1. Decide on the metrics you will measure on an ongoing basis. They should include a combination to measure your forecast accuracy (critical for C-level reporting) as well as measurements that assess the performance of your sales and marketing teams.

2. Determine the cadence for these measurements for weekly, monthly, and quarterly reviews. For most of my career, I used every Friday morning for detailed forecast reviews with my management teams. At this time, I reviewed for each region the revenue commitment, product mix, pipeline movement and growth, marketing performance, and individual rep performance. Each manager had to come prepared for this review or suffer the embarrassment of conducting a similar review the following Monday. If an executive had an important client meeting (always an acceptable excuse), then he or she would have a representative from his or her team to present the data. Since the use of Salesforce.com was a condition of employment for all personnel in my organization, this evaluation process was well automated to eliminate unnecessary work.

3. Each of these meetings would conclude with an assessment of each region's performance versus goals. Regardless of whether a region was exceeding or falling short of their assigned goals, there were people participating on the call from supporting lines of business to offer help. *What*

can we do collectively to help each region be successful? was a key objective of these calls.

4. Ensure your sales operations team prepares for this meeting by comparing monthly and quarterly trending information. Remember—the trend is your friend.

5. Compare your sales and marketing teams against industry benchmarks as much as possible. I have seen sales organizations pat themselves on the back for weekly growth in their conversion ratio only to find out they were twenty points below their competition. There are companies that produce sales productivity analysis reports by industry and business model that you can purchase.

6. Build an executive dashboard that can be distributed to upper management and your team to ensure complete visibility of your business operations. Your team will respond positively that this inspection of their business is a core business process of the company.

These forecast meetings were held every Friday and went beyond assessing the current revenue forecast, key performance metrics tracking, and ensuring assistance from supporting lines of business. These meetings also were held to ensure that sales and marketing resources were working together effectively in each region. Has marketing provided the needed lead flow to make the monthly and quarterly numbers? What sales channels were most successful for each region? What products have been the most successful by region? If any discrepancies in performance exist within regions, it is your responsibility to determine why.

Building an effective and efficient sales organization takes a great deal of work. The professionalism of your sales personnel is a reflection of your professionalism as well. Peter Schultz once said, "Hire character. Train skill." I truly believe in that philosophy. A successful sales executive should not only take great pride in his or her work; a sales representative's reputation is equally if not more important to his or her revenue attainment.

Some of the lessons in this book are not for everybody. Some sales executives use other tools and techniques that work better. For me, my management philosophy, as it pertains to sales, falls under the following themes:

- **Start with strategic clarity**. Everyone must understand his or her individual contributions to the strategic initiatives. Reflect specifics in job descriptions.
- **Train your team well**. Certify sales personnel and partners on the content and messaging regarding our value proposition. Focus on three simple questions: Why should your prospective client do something? Why now? Why with us?
- **Set expectations**. Let the team know what is expected from their role. Make sure everyone understands the importance of not only producing results but also how the results were produced.
- **Hold them accountable**. Inspect the productivity trends that are important to your business and communicate the significance of these measurements to your team.
- **Reward the doers**. Straight from the book titled *Execution—The Discipline of Getting Things Done,* by Larry Bossidy and Ram Charan. Make sure your top performers know they are appreciated. Replacing good people is more expensive and time-consuming than taking care of your best performers in the first place.

Everywhere I have been, these themes have been instrumental to my success. But sales is everybody's responsibility within a company. With that in mind, I encourage people to formulate their own management style that is consistent with the culture of their company. My management style incorporates the following initiatives/beliefs:

- **Collaborative with the functional lines of business**. Teamwork is critical to any success within business, and no salesperson can be successful without the support of each functional line of business. Work closely with legal, finance, and product teams to ensure everyone is committed to maximizing sales and marketing productivity.
- **Overcommunicate**. Make sure the entire company understands the progress of the sales team toward achieving the company's strategic imperatives.
- **Listen to your team**. If I have to make a decision, regardless of whether it will have a positive or negative effect on an organization, I want to hear from the best and brightest on the team. Surround yourself with complementary skills and expertise, and listen to their opinions about the direction of the sales organization.
- **Process disciplines**. Be relentless in implementing productivity initiatives that increase effectiveness and efficiency of your team. The more productive your team is, the more success your organization will recognize.
- **Coach and mentor**. Build your team leadership from within the organization. Show them the path to success. I have been fortunate to work with some of the most talented executives in our industry. They saw something in me and coached me to be the best executive I can be. Pass those lessons along to the next generation.

So what are the key takeaways from this book?

First and foremost that sales predictability is in direct correlation to the level of collaboration between the sales and marketing organization. This is never easy, especially if their goals are not aligned and if they each are measured and compensated differently. Where the sales and marketing relationship hurts the company is when there is a culture of blaming the other organization when things go wrong. Senior leadership can't allow the blame game to happen within their company. Sales and marketing personnel must view each other as teammates with a common goal and not competitors fighting over resources or funding.

We have discussed the pipeline funnel of a company and how marketing and sales contributes individual aspects of the overall revenue cycle. But let me be clear. It is not a marketing or sales pipeline. They share together in the total pipeline and must take complete ownership in its quality and quantity as well as the ability of the company to turn the pipeline into revenue. Throwing leads over the fence does not help anyone. Both organizations need to own the overall revenue cycle.

Improving the working relationship with sales and marketing personnel is paramount to successful sales forecast accuracy. What are specific actions that can contribute to successful collaboration between the two organizations?

- Mutually establish a service level agreement so that each organization is accountable for their specific contribution to the revenue success of the company. This includes clear definition of a quality lead. This also requires a clear definition of a qualified lead. These two definitions must be agreed to by both organizations. It also must be very specific. Measurements must extend down to the individual rep level. How many leads should be expected in a quarter? What is the expected conversion rate for each lead? How much revenue should be sourced from marketing?

- Ensure goals are aligned and forecast accuracy is incorporated into the compensation plans of all sales and marketing personnel. It is also imperative that the goals of each organization are designed to support the other department. Compensation plans must reflect this required teamwork as well as that forecast accuracy is a team effort and a priority of the company.

- Sales should proactively take marketing personnel on sales calls. Show what an ideal prospective client profile looks like, and demonstrate a well-qualified lead can quickly turn into revenue for the company.

- Ensure honest communication through joint meetings. Openly discuss what is working and what needs to improve. Leave egos at the door and come prepared to discuss how to make the company better, not individual departments. Encourage and make it easy for departments to share information.

- Celebrate your mutual success together! Teamwork and collaboration success between sales and marketing organizations is something that should be a source of pride for all department personnel. Celebrate together every sales and marketing milestone.

I hope there was some insight from this book to help you succeed with your future sales and marketing predictability endeavors.

www.ingramcontent.com/pod-product-compliance
Lightning Source LLC
Chambersburg PA
CBHW030750180526
45163CB00003B/966